Adventure Guide to DUBLIN

BORED ALREADY?

WHY NOT...
Get close to a real-dead Crusader?
Train a telescope?
Take off in a glider?
Go to Dublin's Bird Market?
Visit $2^1/_2$ islands?
Measure a conger eel?
Watch bicycle polo?
Find a fossil?
Eat Tex-Mex for breakfast?
Get your hair cut CHEAP?
Pick as many plums as you can eat?
Take a ride on a steam train?
Have a look at a doll's palace?
Cuddle a raccoon?
Meet your own T.D.?
Visit a lighthouse?
Visit a submarine or a sailing ship?
Get published?
Make a record?
Spot a red squirrel three miles from O'Connell Street?
Find your ancestors?
Scrawl on the U2 Wall?
READ ON!

For my parents,
Daniel and Agnes Finn,
who took us places.

The ADVENTURE GUIDE TO DUBLIN

MARY FINN

Illustrated by Frances Hyland

WOLFHOUND PRESS

Third edition 1992

Second edition 1987
First published 1984 by
WOLFHOUND PRESS
68 Mountjoy Square,
Dublin 1.

British Library Cataloguing in Publication Data

Finn, Mary
    The adventure guide to Dublin — 2nd ed.
    1. Amusements — Ireland — Dublin (Dublin) —
    Handbooks, manuals, etc — Juvenile literature
    2. Dublin (Dublin) — Handbooks,
    manuals, etc — Juvenile literature
    1. Title
    790.1'922'0941835   GV1204.467

    ISBN 0-86327-355-6

Cover design and illustration by Aileen Caffrey
Text illustration by Frances Hyland
Typesetting by Wolfhound Press
Printed in the Republic of Ireland by Colour Books, Dublin

CONTENTS

ACKNOWLEDGEMENTS
It's a common story. So many people helped out with ideas, footwork, telephoning and time that I can't attempt to list them, but they know who they are I hope. I thank them.

The person who breathed initial form into the chaos that was this book was Brigid Pike who should really be a co-author only she went to New Zealand leaving behind a trail of bereaved friends.

Dublin Corporation is a body with many faces, all helpful. Thanks especially to the libraries and the Youth Information Centre. All my dealings with the Board of Works were made very pleasant, thanks to Patrick Kavanagh of Northside. Thanks to Mr Stephenson's first and second years in Sandymount High School. Thanks to Daniel Reardon for his poem. And thanks to my Wolfhound editor Loretta Byrne for unfailing good advice and patience.

All my friends put up with me and sometimes offered blandishments: Eileen O'Sullivan typed as well. Ronnie Venables supplied the ultimate support — she minds Daniel.

STARTING POINTS

I started writing this book several years ago when there was only one bee in my bonnet — that was to write a guidebook to Dublin for children. Simple. No one else seemed to have done it. Every other capital city had one.

When I started working on it, the book laid down a few ground rules itself and I found the bonnet contained a few more bees. Rule One ordained that even if parents bought the book it was not to be written for them. Rule Two said design the book for Dubliners rather than visitors because if Dublin children have the freedom of the city that comes from knowing it, well, there'll be all the more life for visiting children anyway.

The bees really began to buzz when various little pieces of Dublin died along the way before publication. If Dublin children really did get to know the character of their city and the store house of things to do, well, they (or their voting parents) might get annoyed at favourite bits dying off. In fact they might make a stink about such things. Favourite beaches for instance. You can get very fond of them. 'Let's keep them okay, in fact let's make them better,' people might say.

So, if you get that sort of hum off the book, it's not imaginary. The hum of the way things could be. The way town planners might think if children had a political lobby. But, most important of all, there was so much to do anyway, that was the best news. All those boring clichés about Dublin's natural advantages — well, they are true. It can be a magical place. I'm delighted to say that you don't have to go to the Antarctic to have an uncharted adventure.

About those expedition chapters — there was no cheating. I did them all, on a bike — and if I could, anyone could. (Bikes became another bonnet bee with me.) But other people don't have to prove anything and can cheat like mad. I wrote the book with independent 9-14-year-olds in mind — but of course it's for anyone that finds it useful. Any of the outings can be a family trip by car for instance, or equally a gang on the bus. Parents of very young children, or parents of handicapped children may think I've glossed over their particular situations, but I think, with the possible exception of the River Trips, everything is open to them also. I hope this is so, and also, that people will contact me about the undoubted treasures I have omitted. Please do. I'd love to know how it goes. And enjoy Dublin!

DOS AND DON'TS

You think Marco Polo didn't have a list of Dos and Don'ts? Of course he did — all survivors do. And since some of the outings in this book involve exploration and scrambling around I've drawn up a very basic survival list. All the accidents hinted at in this list have happened and do happen to people. Don't let them happen to you. And yes, there *are* more Don'ts than Dos, but consider that all the other pages in this book contain a gigantic number of Dos.

GOING

1. DO tell at least one adult exactly where you are going, especially on outdoor trips. Say *how* you are travelling. It's no use leaving a trail of crumbs

2. DON'T go on any long expedition on your own. Even a museum though safe as a house is more fun in company.

OUT AND ABOUT

3. DO bring something satisfying to eat — sweet things lose their appeal on a long trip.

4. DO bring a puncture repair kit (if you cycle!) Buses don't take kindly to sick bicycles and it's *always* a long walk home.

5. DO remember if you bring a small brother or sister, they can't walk as fast or as long as you can, and they get bored easily. Boy, do they get bored. Make sure you have a bit of extra money to distract them.

6. NEVER cross a railway line. You just don't know the timetables and the DART is both fast and quiet-moving.

7. DON'T swim in canals, rivers or reservoirs — they contain weed — or on deserted beaches. Swim parallel to the shore, near to other groups of people.

8. DON'T go into wrecked or just-building houses, they are dangerous.

9. DON'T eat mushrooms or berries even if you're a dab hand in biology.

10. DON'T, if you end up somewhere exotic like a dump — and this is very specific — get into a derelict fridge, wardrobe or anything with a door that can jam shut. People may not hear you.

COMING HOME

11. DON'T hitch-hike unless there are at least twenty of you thumbing the same car. You are *always* within your rights to board a bus or train without even a penny, as long as you give your name and address.

12. NEVER assume that just because it's the end of the day and someone has disappeared, that he/she has gone home. If they don't turn up check with their parents.

Chapter 1

RIVERS AND CANALS

For the outings in this chapter you need a bicycle or two good feet, have to be able to get up early and have lots of stamina to go all day and come back at the end of it.

RIVER TRIPS

You may have a river flowing through your back yard or, better still, underneath your floorboards. You won't find this type of river included here — it is your own, private river and you can trace it to its source yourself and write your own guide. The Poddle river is mapped out in Chapter 4, so forget that for now. Also you won't find any of Dublin's lost rivers in here — such as the Steine or the Pill — they were beyond my powers of description.

TOUR ONE — THE LIFFEY

This tour is shortish, about $3^1/2$ miles from start to the furthest point. It is a go-east-young-person trip, and east in Dublin means dockland. Start from O'Connell Bridge.

If you did a time odyssey on your bicycle back to Viking Dublin, you'd find that the Liffey of this tour was a seashore and you are standing where Vikings went digging for oysters when the tide was out.

Dublin has been creeping downwards ever since, until the mud-green Liffey you see now is a tame beast — smelly too — flowing between nice strong walls. It is still tidal all the way to Watling Bridge by Guinness's brewery, which is quite far into the city. Old photographs

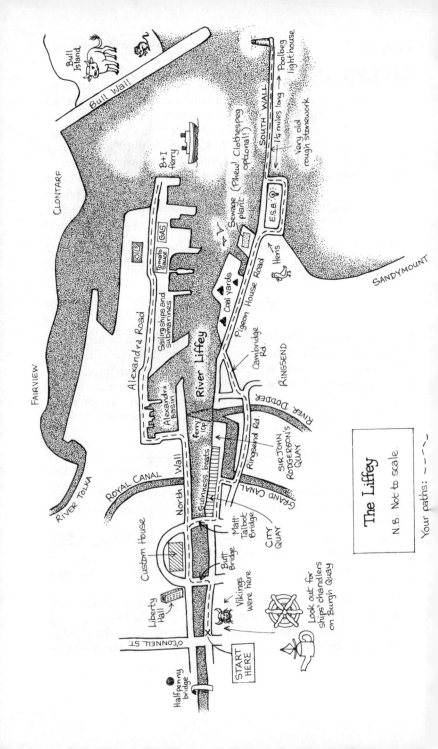

The Liffey

N.B. Not to scale

Your paths: - - - ~ ~

of Dublin show sailing ships' masts just below where you are now. Three more bridges have since been built and they have pushed all the shipping business even further down river.

Going down Burgh Quay on the south side from O'Connell Bridge there is still a ship's chandler — McGowan Verdon. You can buy compasses that work and rather devilish looking sailor's knives in here. Looking up the street towards the Screen cinema and Pearse Street garda station, that little bit of shrubbery in front shows where the river banks reached in Danish Dublin. When the Vikings beached here they put up a Long Stone to show they had claimed the place. (The plaque on the moon is similar if rather more tactful). The Long Stone lasted until the 1790s. The Corn Exchange is the burnt-out building beside the *Irish Press* offices. Its backdoor in Poolbeg Street is giant-sized — have a look. The Corn Exchange was built in 1815 and did just what its name says with all the ships that tied up alongside.

Cross over Butt Bridge and you're on cobblestones, bumpy if you're on a bike but they don't stretch far. Liberty Hall, the little piece of Manhattan on your left, was built in 1965. It's the home of many trade unions, just like the first Liberty Hall which was burnt down in 1916. The 'new' Custom House is on your right.

James Gandon designed this Custom House and building started in 1791. The people who were supposed to benefit from the new Custom House, tradesmen and merchants, were furious because it seemed to them at too great a distance from the city. (It was outside Burgherland). So they hired a mob to fill in the foundation trenches. The weather turned out grand and sunny so the mob gave up and swam in the trenches instead. But Gandon carried a sword whenever he came to visit the site — just in case.

The Custom House is built of granite and Portland stone and cost about half a million pounds — an awful lot in those days. It was burnt in 1921 but the outside was mostly unharmed. So you can see the river gods' heads on the frieze. Custom then and now meant imports and exports and cattle were big business; look out for the friendly bulls' heads over the centre pillars. At the back of the Custom House are four statues representing Europe, Asia, Africa and America. There is not even a kangaroo from Australia, but no prizes for guessing why not.

Cross back over the river on the Matt Talbot Memorial Bridge. The blue and cream Guinness boats are always the first moorings in

Dublin port, just below the Matt Talbot Bridge. If you get there at the right time, watch the streamlined loading procedure. Nowadays great Guinness tankers pump their cargo aboard; they replace the horse drays and their barrels which were still in business twenty years ago. Officially no one is allowed on board, but you never know your luck. (See Guinness Hopstore, page 71)

At Matt Talbot Bridge you have a choice of routes — the North Wall or the South Wall. You could make a real meal of the Liffey and do both on the same day, but I would recommend two different tours.

RIVER TRIPS — NORTH WALL

By bike you should definitely be accompanied by an adult, traffic or no traffic, because you're entering dock area. Car is the best mode for this odd little trip. This is the side of the river that has deep sea docks. It's also a side that has a large tile shop, so if parents drag offspring to walk around a tile shop they could make up for it by going further downriver afterwards.

After the Custom House you'll see the huge financial buildings development: it's similar but much tinier than the river development on the Thames in London. You can spot where the Royal Canal flows into the Liffey — it's where the dinosaurs of dock cranes stand. Continue down to the Point. This huge concert/theatre building was developed from warehouses. It's got a heli-pad for rock stars now; it used to have a running goods railway.

Turn left at the roundabout and head down for the docks. There are two entrances: at Alexandra Road or a few hundred yards up — you can take either. Once you get past the custom police you will have one of the weirdest trips possible in Dublin. Everywhere there are oil tanks, gas tanks, warning notices — it's like a radio-active settlement on the moon. Not at all pretty but you can get an unusual view of the city ticking over. At the end you can see the two arms of Dublin port stretched out — the North Bull Wall with its starboard green light-house trying to touch the port-red Poolbeg lighthouse on the South Wall.

The ferries leave from here, and further back towards the city, at Alexandra Basin, are the docks for visiting monsters. Navy ships, submarines and sail training ships from many nations call on occa-sional courtesy calls and some have conducted tours. These are advertised in the papers, though it's usually the sailors in uniform around the city centre that are the giveaway. Head back as you came. The custom police will probably wave you through, but then you could be a smuggler...

THE SOUTH WALL

Continue on down the dockside — be careful, the traffic is fast here because this is a southside shortcut. This district is called City Quay. All the pubs along here have a special licence to open at seven o'clock in the morning for the dockworkers. Look out for Dockers and the Eight Bells. Behind Dockers is Windmill Lane. Go down here to make the pilgrimage to the U2 Wall. For years fans have been writing strange and wonderful messages on the walls beside Windmill recording studios, first home of the Dublin band. Have a read and add a bit if you have the equipment. Fishing boats and the Irish Navy's *Granuaile* usually dock on Sir John Rogerson's Quay. The very tip of the quay is where the Liffey ferry made its triangular trip between 1386 and 1984. Then (since this book first appeared) the powers that be zapped it and built the new toll bridge downriver instead. It's free for walkers and cyclists but cars have to pay 50p. A toll may be a nice medieval notion but the former ferry that cost 10p was much nicer again.

Go round the Grand Canal Basin, (See Windsurfing, page 140) onto Ringsend Road and into Ringsend village. On the way are huge dilapidated warehouses and factories — look out for the Tropical Fruit Company, the National Ice and Cold Storage Company Limited, old Boland's Mills — which will remind you how busy the Grand Canal must have been in its heyday.

Turn left at Ringsend village into Thorncastle Street and right into Cambridge Road and on to Pigeonhouse Road. Ringsend village used to be a small fishing village cut off from the city of Dublin by the marshes round the mouth of the Dodder. In the 1600s, however, a pier was built out along where you are now, and all the ships which used to dock in Dalkey harbour landed here. The giant candy-stick in front of you, the Pigeonhouse power station, was not called after a flock of homing pigeons, but after an enterprising gentleman named Mr. Pidgeon (though the spelling is not the same). He built a hotel on the pier so that tired travellers could stay the night before braving the journey across the Dodder slobs towards Dublin. This had to be done in a special, tough vehicle called a Ringsend Carr.

Pigeonhouse Road is beautiful to walk or cycle along because you are slap up against the river wall with ships, dredgers and tugs going by almost at your elbow. If you do not believe there is a number 1 bus, well, this is its stamping ground — it goes to the power station. At the end of the terrace of houses you pass a group of ruined dwellings which was where the coastguards used to live. Further on are the coal yards — you can pick up a good stock of fuel from droppings on the road. You come to a smelly area which is the sewage treatment plant. The gulls love it. There is not so much for them in the Pigeonhouse military fort which you ride through. You can still see the remains of the walls and some of the garrison houses are still lived in. The soldiers who lived here were scavengers themselves, notably in the 1790s. Unfortunate locals were pressganged on several occasions and taken on board ship for fighting in destinations abroad. Ringsend Robin Hoods rescued quite a few of them in hold-ups.

Ahead of you now are the gates of the power station and in its grounds you can see the original Pigeonhouse. Groups can visit the station (See Inside Jobs, page 103) but right now go round it, past the dump, past the rocks and on to the start of the South Wall proper.

Going out on the wall is an experience not to be missed. It's a tiny road that goes two miles right out into the middle of Dublin Bay, the most isolated part of the city with its lighthouse at the end. This has been here since 1761. The flagstones are rough on bikes, you really must walk out. The journey seems more like a boat ride than a walk, and you have the best 'outside looking in' view of the city and port. You will see all sorts of sea birds: cormorants, terns, oystercatchers. There is excellent sea-fishing from the rocks for mackerel, bass, eel and sea-trout. Don't go out on a rough day, and come back the way you went!

TOUR TWO — THE DODDER

This trip takes you from the mouth of the Dodder river to its source in the Dublin mountains (a distance of roughly 15 miles), so whatever else you do, bring *food* and *boots*. You'll need our map or a better one (O.S. 16). It's really worth going the whole way, because if you ever get stuck with a bore who's climbed Everest or traced the Nile to its source, the Dodder trip could be your best attack.

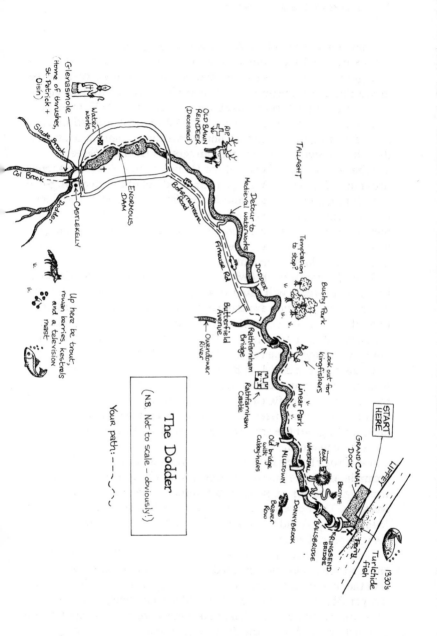

The Dodder

(N.B. Not to scale – obviously!)

Your path:- - - - ∿∿∿

Glenasmole
(Home of thrushes,
St. Patrick + Oisín)

Slade Brook

Col Brook

Dodder

CASTLEKELLY

Water-
works

OLD BAWN
REINDEER
(Deceased)

RIP

TALLAGHT

ENORMOUS
DAM

Bohernabreena
Road

Firhouse Rd

Detour to
Medieval waterworks

DODDER

Owendoher
River

Butterfield
Avenue

Rathfarnham
Bridge

Rathfarnham
Castle

Temptation
to stop?

Bushy Park

Look out for
kingfishers

Linear Park

Old bridge
with cubby-holes

MILLTOWN

WEIR

WATERFALL

BEAVER
ROW

DONNYBROOK

BALLSBRIDGE

WEIR

RINGSEND
BRIDGE

BECTIVE

GRAND CANAL
DOCK

START
HERE

Ferry

LIFFEY

Turlehide
fish

1330's

Up here be trout,
rowan berries, kestrels
and a television
mast

There's a meeting of the waters of the Liffey, the Grand Canal and the Dodder and that's your starting point. You cross Ringsend Bridge (straight out from Pearse Street) and go left down Thorncastle Street to see this H_2O junction. The Grand Canal docks are just facing. There's a tale that during a great medieval famine in 1331, monstrous fish called Turlchides, between 30 and 40 feet long, turned up right here. Presumably Ringsend fishermen caught them and brought them to be carved into Turlchideburgers in Fishamble Street.

What is no fishy tale is that the Dodder in those days was much wider and shallower, making a marshland out of the area. Ringsend Carrs, bringing passengers and parcels from the Pigeonhouse docks, used to splash through merrily before any bridges were built. When they were finally built, the Dodder bridges had a habit of floating out to sea in rough weather. Even now, in spells of bad weather, the Dodder gets a mean swell on it.

Take the south bank (left, if that's any help) from Ringsend to Ballsbridge, which will bring you under the railway and past Lansdowne rugby grounds. Near the bridge at Ballsbridge and further up river at Herbert Park you'll see some of the small, pretty, redbrick cottages that are found all over Dublin 4. They were built seventy to ninety years ago as part of the Pembroke estate.

Cross over the bridge at Ballsbridge to the north bank and go by what was Johnston Mooney and O'Brien's bakery and mills. Parts of the bakery look quite ancient, and there were stables until quite recently for its horse fleet. Before the bakery there was a calico works here, turning out the stuff that small girls' and house-maids' pinafores were made of.

Go up by Herbert Park. Near Donnybrook bridge is Bective sports grounds, once the site of the Great Mad Crazy Donnybrook Fair, which gave a lot of people sore heads every August from 1204 onwards. The noise was too much for one sensible Victorian lion in 1846: he escaped and rolled around like a puppy in the Dodder before being captured again.

Find the bridge. You can either go up Beaver Row on the south bank, a pretty country-type road, or if you want to mess with water take the path on the north side, by crossing the iron footbridge. You can get down to the first of the Dodder weirs here, and there's an accessible weedy island. Good in droughty weather for climbing on and getting up close to the duck families that are learning to swim, and in wet weather the weir looks pretty spectacular.

At Clonskea take either bank to Milltown. On this stretch of river from Clonskea as far as Old Bawn in Tallaght there used to be fifty mills and factories using Dodder water power. There were flour mills, iron works, woollen mills, cotton and saw mills. The more you can get right down to the banks, the more of the stubs of these old mills, and their mill races, you will find. You can plot them on your own map of the Dodder.

Milltown has two bridges. The old one, a medieval one, doesn't lead anywhere any more, but it's in perfect shape and has a pedestrian cubby-hole where in bygone days you dived for cover as a Hell's Angel dogcart tried to ram you. There are actually three bridges if you count the huge railway viaduct; the Nine Arches which carried the Harcourt Line, alas, is no longer used, but it *may* be revived.

Go up the hill by the Dropping Well pub, and turn left at the top, down the curvy old road past North's factory to the river again. This is the beginning of the Dodder Linear Park that goes all the way to Bushy Park and Templeogue Bridge. Here river birds begin in earnest though kingfishers and herons have been seen as far down as Donnybrook and Ballsbridge. On the road alongside, one of the old gates to Rathfarnham Castle sits in the middle of nowhere. The original castle was built because Rathfarnham was not a safe place to live at all. Dublin and Wicklow chieftains operated a Patriotic Front with Bonny and Clyde-type raids on the Pale, and one of their chief haunts was Rathfarnham. However, there's only one ghost on record here, a retriever that drowned in a pond, and if you want to look for it, go ahead. The Castle has been acquired by the Office of Public Works and after restoration will be opened to the public.

You can criss-cross the river on bridges and stepping-stones all along the way to Rathfarnham Bridge. Fishing is popular here — check with the Dodder Angling Association. (See Angling, page 138) Cross over Rathfarnham Bridge and go on as before. The Owendower river joins the Dodder here, and the Linear Park ends at the next bridge but you can carry on. Bushy Park, on the right, is a decent park, but for river tracking purposes your first ordeal is on the left — on the south bank. It involves following the river instead of the comfy road. There's a track, but you will have to carry your bike over a gate. If you are a good navigator you will end up in Butterfield Avenue. Then you can wheel down the hill, straight through the next crossroads and along Firhouse Road. It's a goodish way to the next glimpse of water but it's easy cycling. (Of course if you had big waders, you'd not have to leave the river at all, but deep water is on its way anyway, you'll see.)

At the Firhouse Inn there's a little housing estate. Go round the back and you'll see another Dodder waterfall with a footbridge across. Next thing is a small stream but that's exactly what it's not. Right here in 1244 the Sheriff of Dublin said 'Dig' and they dug. They dug right across the fields to Tallaght and made a channel between the Dodder and the Poddle. You can see it take off here with its ancient stonework and strange sluiceworks and you can follow its course on a map. The reason for it was that there simply wasn't enough water in Dublin for everyone to have their yearly scrub. The city of Dublin kept growing and the poor little Poddle did its best but it just wasn't big enough. This little stream — called the City Watercourse — made an enormous difference, and everyone was happy for another 500 years.

Back and on to Old Bawn. Old Bawn House, on the right, is a real humdinger. Apparently coaches with headless horses and horsemen drop by regularly and deposit an archbishop (with a head) who makes a quick tour of the premises he built here in 1630, and then they all head off again. Out in the back of Old Bawn House, by the river, there were some grim executions in 1816. You can see the mantelpiece from poor Old Bawn House in the 1916 room in the National Museum, and a hoary old thing it is too.

Off again down Bohernabreena Road to the Bridge. The Dodder is very strong here, full of bounce and vigour, coming out of the Bohernabreena reservoir. The entrance to the reservoir and waterworks is just over the bridge, and you are officially allowed in with a special pass from Dublin Corporation.

If you get in, keep to the right or west side of the lakes. You are not allowed to swim in them but you can fish. There are two enormous dams — well, nearly enormous — with streams, pipes and gurglings everywhere. The waterworks was built in 1883 — but it is classy and perfect for exploring. There's a grassy slope down from the dam that is heaven to roll down, no matter how silly it all looks.

The whole river valley looks like a little piece of Canada, especially in autumn, but as far as stories go it was one of the first places in Ireland to be inhabited. The valley is called Glenasmole, the Valley of the Thrushes — and if you believe everything that's in print, well whistle a certain tune and Fionn MacCumhail and Oisín and the rest of the pack will come bounding out of the bushes. Bohernabreena was a magic fort with gorgeous food, and Glenasmole was one of their favourite pads, and indeed, as far as Oisín was concerned, it was nothing less than Texas. Oisín met St. Patrick who had a very mean housekeeper. The housekeeper served them scraps rather than a meal. Oisín was highly insulted and mooned over Glenasmole where, he claimed, the rowan berries were bigger than bread rolls, the ivy was bigger again, and the blackbirds were the size of St. Patrick's roast beef dinner. You can check out his claim for yourself.

If you've waited until now to eat, eat by the lakes. The water is so still, especially on misty days, that all those Fianna at the bottom of the lake are just too lazy to hold a sword up.

That done, you might like to go right round to the far side of the lakes and search out the ancient church and well of a saint called Santan. Or stick to the main entrance at the top of the valley. You're on the Castlekelly road — go left and up. On the right you'll see a stile beyond which is a forestry clearance road. The mountain is ahead of you, and if you look at the map you'll see the problem, which has been carefully kept from you till now.

Which is the real Dodder? Does it matter? I followed the middle stream, Cot Brook, up river by shingle pools, rowan trees and gold (it looked like) in the river bed. And, yes, I did see the stream pop out of the bog, just like the books say, quite near to the television mast. But be warned: it is at least a two-hour trek from the road up and back, so if you want to leave this journey until another day don't feel ashamed. *Don't* go up on a foggy day — you could easily get lost, and for the same reason *make sure* you've told several people exactly where you're going.

THE CANALS

The Northside has one (the Royal), so has the Southside (the Grand) so there can be no fighting. But the south had theirs first (in 1779), then the north stole the Grand's old blueprints and plotted the Royal from them. So the Al Capone among canals is the Royal. But because the two canals were so close to each other all the way to the Shannon, neither of them could get an upper edge on the market of passengers and goods. Each had its big barges pulled along — this was before steam, remember — by horses nearly as big. If you've read *The Wind in the Willows* it's all in there. The last straw for the canals, that saved umpteen tow-horses' backs, was the railways.

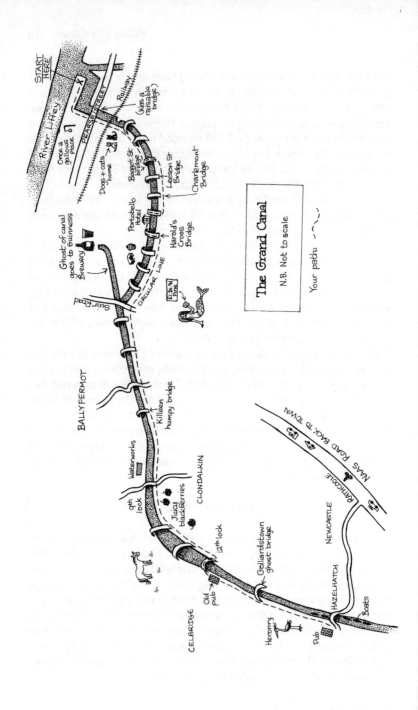

But as everyone who crosses either of the canals on their way to town knows, they are far from dead, what with fishing, canoeing, swimming in summer and the war between the dumpers and the cleaner-uppers. Since most of us have a horizontal relationship with the canals it's no harm to try a vertical one for a change, and travel along the towpaths. Bikes are essential if you want to cover all the ground at once, but don't pick a day after a run of rainy weather unless you've got wellingtons, chains on your wheels and an extraordinarily sunny temper. Pick a good dry day — up-canal these towpaths are still what most roads once were: dirt-tracks.

TOUR THREE — THE GRAND CANAL

Get right down to where the Grand Canal enters the Liffey, going down the south quays till you can go no further. The canal docks are a splendid place in their own way, with strange outlets and locks and a great open harbour that gets used for boatbuilding, windsurfing and canoeing. Be very careful though if you decide to spend some time exploring these ways and looking at the poor hulks of boats — *rotting wood is dangerous stuff*. With one ounce of imagination this area could be one of the most beautiful parts of any city, full of small workshops, houseboats and restaurants, including a children's area, as in the very popular Camden Docks in London. (You could write to Dublin Corporation or any of the Dublin 4 TDs to ask why not).

Meanwhile the canal may not look its prettiest — but don't be put off, it's come a journey of 80 odd miles from the Shannon to here. The grimy buildings along the way are among Dublin's oldest industrial ones — Hammond Lane, Bolands and the Gas Company with its hills of coal and gasometers and whatever happens between the two of them that makes gas. Look out for a street called Misery Hill, which was once a leper colony, and then a gallows place. If you stare down at the middle of the wide bridge (Pearse Street) you can see that it could be raised once — the joints are still there.

Leave the docks part of the Grand Canal and travel up on the north or right-hand side. This part of the canal, from Ringsend to Rialto, was really an afterthought. It's called the Circular Line and you can see why if you look at it on a map, though travelling up-canal on the bike it seems as straight as a ruler.

You come up towards Baggot Street and Leeson Street bridges. You meet your first lock with the prim notice 'Not for Public Use'.

There are thirty-six locks all the way to the Shannon, with the canal ascending to Robertstown, Co. Kildare, and level or descending after that. You may see the water-levels being changed in the locks; there's a greater chance of doing so in summer when cruisers use the canal.

Lock-keepers had a hard enough time in the early days — if a dead dog floated past they had to fish it out and bury it in their own gardens. As well as that they were each provided with a halbert to cope with vandals or patriotic saboteurs. There was plenty of that, especially outside the city: canal banks broken open, boats smashed, with the miserable shareholders of the Grand Canal Company watching their stocks fluctuating for real. But the lock-keepers were also supposed to guard against simpler kinds of behaviour. Swimming or washing in the canal brought a fine of £1.2s.9d., and if your dog did the same, well, eleven shillings was the wet money due. The canal was opened over 200 years ago, in February 1779 to be exact, and in those days that was pretty hefty money. Needless to say, offenders were not easily caught.

Most boat-handlers operate the locks themselves these days. There's a special 'key' that opens the sluices in the top lock. This lets the water through to fill the bottom so that it becomes level. A load of hand power is needed to push the gates open and the boats can then pass up or down. If there's a number of boats passing each other the operation takes quite a while, but nobody expects speed on canal ways. It's good fun to watch, or to give a hand with pushing or holding a rope.

Go up the picture-bookish stretch of canal between Mount Street and Leeson Street. Patrick Kavanagh the poet, whose memorial seat is by Baggot Street lockgates, wrote lovingly of the place. He probably knew by name the goats that were tethered here once, on long iron chains.

On up to Charlemont bridge and Portobello. The handsome dark green building, picked out in white, was once one of the Grand Canal Grand Hotels. There were four others, at Sallins, Robertstown, Tullamore and Shannon Harbour. Even though stage-coaches were quicker, eighteenth- and nineteenth-century passengers liked the comfort and tranquillity of canal travel. It certainly was no candidate for speed warfare, not even for a water rat race. Early speeds averaged 2 mph, settled later at 4 mph, and when fly boats (narrower, with more frequent changes of horse) were introduced, a dazzling 9 mph was reached. (No one nowadays can imagine just how many horses were around in pre-engine days, but as a general rule, it was impossible to walk 100 yards without tripping over several horses. Even when you were on a boat.)

If you intend to follow the canal trail further, here at Portobello is a good place to pick some fruit, have some chocolate or sandwiches, because you will need them. Canal passengers had mainly mutton and spud stews, kept on the boil in huge cauldrons. The boats — their seats were filled with chopped hay — were capable of carrying '15 uncrinolined passengers'.

Shake an uncrinolined leg there and continue on the north bank, round the Institute of Education and up Portobello Road, full of tiny redbrick cottages, past the abattoir to Clanbrassil Street bridge, where it's all change to the south bank, and stick to that side until further notice. There is an ancient barge moored beside Griffith Barracks; it's the same shape as the Guinness barges.

When you come to Suir Road bridge, you will see a dead canal on your right. This was the straight and narrow branch that once led into the heart of the city — to the Grand Canal Basin, Basin Lane and the Pipes. The Pipes of course led to Guinness's brewery; Guinness were the last commercial users of the canal, with barges afloat until 1950.

Continue on a comfortable towpath up Davitt Road — the next bridge gives you a path that will train you in bike-scrambling. Here also is a very cute and easily spotted lock-house with its own footbridge, and between here and Killeen's humpy bridge there are often several friendly and curious wandering horses.

Bridges are few from now on, so be sure you want to go on once you've passed one — there's no accessible road from the towpath. This route conducts you as far as Hazelhatch (in Co. Kildare) but you can drop off at two points: Clondalkin, or the 12th lock on the Lucan Road. *Hint:* On a fine autumn day you can't beat this section of the canal and there are millions of juicy unclaimed blackberries.

Clondalkin and Ballyfermot were villages far from the centre of activities in canal-travelling days. Passengers would have felt rural by now, travelling west. By the canal it still feels that way. Dublin Corporation has waterworks on the north bank before Clondalkin — after Clondalkin, whatever you do, don't take the north bank (on a bike at any rate). It may look more tempting but after the locks there's a dead end.

It's quite a stretch up to the 12th lock (you'll know it by the old pub) and here the advice changes. Cross *now* to the north bank, go down by the mill and the pub, squeeze your bike past the gate, and you're into the wildest and loveliest stretch of the canal as far as Hazelhatch. 12th lock and Hazelhatch have several moored house-boats which give them an air of watery business. You'll pass under a derelict bridge at Golliardstown. Nearby is a waterlogged quarry: *ignore it, quarries are dangerous places because they can subside.* There are many waterbirds to be seen here: herons and moorhens abound. There's a prickly stretch just before Hazelhatch which you have to grin and bear, and then you have arrived. A grand total of 13 miles from Ringsend that would have taken you $3^1/2$ hours in a horse-drawn canal boat. How long did it take you?

You can return the same way. If that's not a good idea, turn left to Celbridge/Lucan, or right to Newcastle/Clondalkin, and then the main roads lead to town.

TOUR FOUR — THE ROYAL CANAL

This trip from start to furthest point is approximately 13 miles. Returning by the main road is shorter. The Royal Canal has had a bad deal — although it's being restored at present — but it's got certain advantages over the Grand:

1. It's easier going for a start. I had to leave the towpath once but that was because of wet weather beforehand. Walkers can march straight through.

2. You get out of the city much more quickly.

3. It's got more character.

Take the north quays, past the Custom House down to Spencer Dock where the Royal joins the Liffey without any fancy docks at all. Go up Guild Street and leave the canal, straight down Seville Place to where the Five Lamps are and join it again at the North Strand bridge. You can take the towpath from now on.

For a while now the canal is going to look a bit like a dead fish — sometimes you have to stare right down to see if there is any canal left at all. But even before the canal this place was a bit off. North Strand was literally a strand once and this part of the city — up to the next road at Ballybough — was known as Mud Island. Gangsters, smugglers and conmen of the pimpliest kind lived in rows of cabins here in a flea-loud glade. There was even a king of Mud Island, a kind of Fagin character, and if you got the thumbs down from him you'd shortly be found in a Mud Island dustbin. When some of the sea was

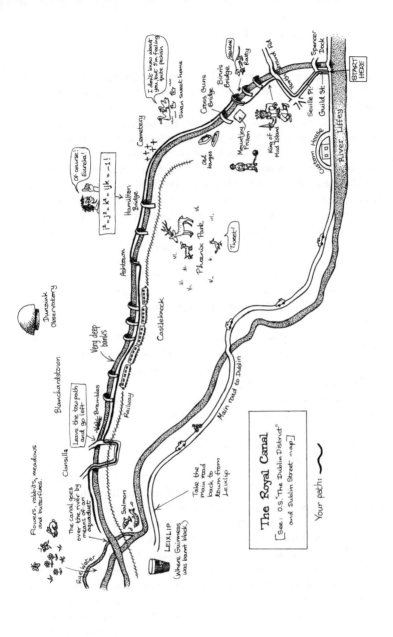

reclaimed and new roads built in the eighteenth century, Mud Island said goodbye. But meanwhile don't look too closely at anything suspicious.

On your way up to Binn's bridge at Drumcondra you'll probably see, as I did, several rats swimming. Whatever you feel about rats, they certainly don't look as unsavoury in the open, and they are wonderful swimmers, like tiny beavers. Binn's bridge has a fine clear nameplate on it — most of the other bridges' names are difficult to read, but all of them are called after directors of the Royal Canal Company. Mr. Binns was the one supposed to be responsible for stealing the Grand's plans. But it took a long time to get the canal going — you see 1795 on this bridge but it was not finished until 1817, and it never did anything like the amount of business the Grand did.

After Binn's bridge take the right or north bank. You can really feel the climb along the Royal, which of course is why the locks are so deep. It will be good to see it open again — it's been closed to navigation, except for get-around canoes, since 1961.

The enormous place on your left is Mountjoy Prison which is why the song goes: 'The aul' triangle goes jingle jangle / Along the banks of the Royal Canal'. Around the jail runs a ditch of water which turns it into a fortressy-looking place.

Halfway down is the only lock you'll get a bicycle across without problems, and past Mountjoy you'll see another dead canal. This grassy bank goes all the way down to Broadstone Railway station, which is dead too, come to think of it. Passengers for boats to Mullingar got on here (if they paid for their dogs, a first-class service was laid on for the beasts). If you go across the North Circular Road, in search of a place called Royal Canal Bank, you *will* find water — a kind of secret pond with resident water birds. Ironically, this was part of a waterworks, and nothing to do with the canal.

Across the big bridge, Cross Guns bridge, and down the towpath again. Mills old and new are settled in here for the duration. So are certain others — in the cemetery on the right with its fooled-you round tower, built for Daniel O'Connell's monument. (See page 88)

It's very pleasant from now on with the trains trundling by to Galway and you whizzing by on your bike. A swan family, with an almost zero population growth of two elegant cygnets, can usually be found outside some cottages here on the towpath. They're grateful for scraps. Mostly the path goes under the humpy bridges and lets the roads go by overhead. Look out for Hamilton's bridge — it's clearly marked on the far side. A scholarly bod indeed was William Rowan Hamilton. While most people would be digesting their rice krispies on the way to work, his brain was digesting higher mathematics. Going under this bridge one morning in 1843 on his way to Dunsink Observatory he said 'Eureka!' and came out with: $1^2 = J^2 = K^2 = ijk = -1$. Whatever that means, it's apparently Very Important and known as a Quaternion Equation. And it's carved on the bridge.

You're on the south bank after Ashtown and the canal becomes very beautiful indeed. Between Castleknock and Clonsilla it tries to find Australia. Well, just look how far below you it is. This stretch had to be dug through solid rock; it was known as the Deep Sinking and you'll find the rock coming through the towpath. You can imagine the length of rope that the poor horses needed in order to tow. Don't fall in!

At the next level crossing — the bridge before Clonsilla — change sides again. (And there's a beautiful garden in Clonsilla called Shackleton's, see page 96) At Clonsilla you may need a road direction because the path is quite brambly. Turn left where the signpost says: 'Lucan 3 miles', and follow the main road to the next signpost. Turn right where you know the canal should be and hey-presto it is. The detour is about a mile. You can continue the rest of the way to Rye Valley which is where you stop.

This is how you know Rye Valley. It's a bit like the riddle of the duck's egg, going over water and under water. The water (canal) goes over the water (the Rye) by way of a water bridge or aqueduct. These were not easy to make, believe me, even if Roman aqueducts were in mass production all over Europe. Far below you see the Rye sparkling in its own valley, and you can scramble down to the waterfall if you like. It will lead you to the water-meadows which are a botanist's dream. They're full of wild flowers every spring and summer — purple valerian, tickly teasel, smelly lady's bed-straw, guelder roses, and grass of Parnassus are some of the delicately-coloured flowers you find here. Rabbits are around also, and all kinds of butterflies.

At the bridge, leave the canal and turn left back into Leixlip. Leixlip is the name the Vikings gave to this stretch of country. Lax-hlaup means salmon leap, which they had to do here if they wanted to get up-river and spawn.

The small Church of Ireland on the main street is over 1,000 years old and was part of a fort in those days. Say hello to the face on the tower — it's been around long enough.

The graveyard is nice and old too, and across the river is Leixlip Castle, owned by a Guinness, which is all right because the first Guinness brewery was next door to the Church in what is now the parking lot. In those old days Guinness was not brown and creamy, it was common old pale ale. The story goes that one day the head brewer fell asleep and burnt the day's quota of pale ale. He fed it to the local peasantry who kept coming back for more of the lovely burnt stuff.

If you go to the end of the parking lot you'll see the Leixlip Castle Folly facing you. Someone has painted a strange lady with a lute on one window singing to the Liffey at Leixlip for ever.

So, it's time to head homewards. Look out for the drainpipe house at the end of the village. If you take the main road back be careful — best to cycle on the path. Or you can take the road for Clonsilla, Blanchardstown and the Phoenix Park — it's signposted all the way.

Chapter 2
SHOPPING

This section is about spending money — yours. It's a random and off-beat guide to shopping, because I presume you have the bare necessities but are interested in cheap, unusual or extra-pleasant places to go. So, for instance, clothes shops are not included, but fancy dressing up is. And, apart from truly specialist shops, this chapter sticks close to the city centre. Your local shopping centre may have nearly everything, but you can't beat a good lazy day in town, and you certainly won't find the variety of odd-bod places in the suburbs. So, gather a gang some Saturday, call in your assets and head downtown. Bus is best for a shopping trip.

ANCESTORS

You can almost buy ancestors. If you like your family name and/or have relations visiting from America, a good place to go is a heraldic artist's shop. They have maps, crests, scrolls, histories, badges, songs. Try Heraldic Artists in Nassau Street or Historic Families, Fleet Street.

A map of Ireland with family names on it is on sale in most bookshops and, of course, the crème de la crème of heraldic places is the Genealogical Office in Kildare St. (See page 52)

ARTY-CRAFTY

Two good all-round art shops are The Drawing Centre in South Leinster Street and Kennedy's in Harcourt Street. They are for professionals so they are expensive. The Art and Hobby Shop on the top floor of the Stephen's Green Centre is good for younger people.

Eason's second floor will tog out anyone who's not too demanding, with oils, posterpaints, millions of markers and lots of types of paper. Mulvany Brothers the picture framers on Wellington Quay will also supply you with papers and paints. The pictures in the window might give you some ideas. Arnott's in Henry Street has acres of bright poppy felt and miles of raffia. (For art classes see page 123)

BALLET

If you take up any kind of dance, or if you just like the gear, Dance World in Parnell Street will fit you out, in tights, shoes and tulle. Most department stores also stock leotards and dance tights. (For dance classes see page 124)

BICYCLES

Bicycles almost deserve a chapter on their own because they figure so prominently in this guidebook.

If you're buying a bike, make sure you get a good try-out first and, if you're not comfortable, don't take the bike just because it looks good. Lots of people love racers, mountain bikes and BMX but if you don't feel comfortable on one (or the price isn't right) try out the other reliables. Many shops sell second-hands which means some kind of guarantee; the alternative is to try the evening papers or local papers.

A dynamo, carrier and pump are the best accessories to get. Saddle-bags and panniers can be very expensive; you'll find large sports bags in Dunne's Stores that do just as well and are much cheaper. And get a good lock and chain. A combination lock is the least bother unless you have a rotten memory. Always lock the gear wheel and the frame to a fixed object and always in as public a place as possible. 'They' can manage much better in dark lanes.

However, since the city centre is full of professional thieves with equipment, once you've bought a bike, insure it at once. If your family has house contents insurance it's only a couple of pounds extra to get a bicycle mentioned in the policy.

Reliable city stockists are: MacDonald's in Wexford Street, Penny-farthing in Aungier Street, Hardings of Bachelors Walk, The Bike Store at 58 Lower Gardiner Street and Cycleways in Parnell Street. Suburban dealers are just as good and may have a wider selection of second-hands or hire-purchase terms.

You can park your bike in town in absolute safety by leaving it with the Square Deal Cycleworks, Temple Lane, off Dame Street, for a very small fee. For twilight or night cycling, you must be properly lit up; the best thing is to get your bicycle fitted with a dynamo. Otherwise, front and back lights have to be removed. You should get yourself fitted too with reflective armbands and/or belts.

Hiring bicycles: Many shops have a special Rent-a-Bike scheme with daily and weekly rates. A deposit and proper identification are required. You can get a list of all the stockists who operate this scheme from Dublin Tourism in O'Connell Street. An Oige (See page 140) do a very cheap bike plus hostel voucher holiday for members.

BOOKSHOPS

Bookshops are all round the city so first I will mention the ones that have second-hand departments because these buy from you as well as sell to you. You won't make very much but you can get rid of any old books you no longer want, for a profit.

On the south quays near the Ha'penny Bridge is Webb's. They have prints and maps as well, and lots of ancient-looking cheap books. Nassau Street has Fred Hanna's (downstairs is second-hand) and, at the far end, in Clare Street, is Greene's. It is a beautiful shop, with a book-thronged staircase and it has appeared in many films set in Dublin. But it may have bad memories for you because it also stocks schoolbooks. Chapters Bookshop in Henry Street also buy books secondhand.

The Mansion House in Dawson Street sells books and comics — now and again. Sales of Work are sometimes held in the Round Room, and every so often a Book Barrow Fair is announced in the papers. These fairs are a throw-back to the days when the Liffey quays were full of book merchants selling from barrows, like they still do in Paris.

Books a little out of the common run you will find at the following: The Forbidden Planet in Dawson Street is given over to comicbooks. Old and new classics are here, along with kits (make your own Alien), figures, t-shirts and even how-to-draw-like-comicbooks books. The Alchemist's Head in Dame Street stocks science fiction, fantasy and a lot of American comics. There is an Irish language bookshop at 6 Harcourt Street. They have very cheap, gloriously illustrated picture books that will make younger members of the family very happy.

In Dawson Street Hodges Figgis and Waterstone's are open late every evening and they're also open on Sundays. Eason's has a well-stocked children's department and a play area for small children. They also have a bargain shop downstairs which has an amazing selection of new books dirt cheap.

Children's Book Week (fortnight actually) is in October every year, with happenings, writers in person and competitions in all bookshops that stock children's books.

FANCY DRESS

Bourke's at 64 Dame Street near the Olympia Theatre caters especially for fancy dress. It's a professional costumier shop and a great place to burrow around. They also stock stage make-up of every kind. But you can make your own fancy dress out of bright bits and pieces. Second-hand clothes and curtains are the basics, and tinsel, sequins, gold and silver paint are the transformers.

For the basics try the Simon Shop in Camden Street, Oxfam in South King Street, or Eager Beaver or Damascus in Crown Alley, Temple Bar. Army Bargains in Little Mary Street off Capel Street have bits of uniforms and belts and equipment. Art and model shops have gold and silver paint. Indian shops sell exotic scarves and shawls which make great costumes. There's one in the ILAC Centre, and others can be found in Liffey Street, Wicklow Street and Grafton Street.

For very classy things try Jenny Vander's in South Great George's Street Arcade. They have beautiful antique clothes, including children's clothes. Very dear, but good for ideas.

Any library will have books on costume — ask at the counter.

FOOD

Most of us eat wherever we happen to find ourselves, but nevertheless there are places worth going to on special occasions. Try this list.

Burger and milkshake freaks will already have their favourite marked out from the selection of McDonald's, Burgerland and Burger King eating dens. They offer great basic junk chomping in Grafton Street, O'Connell Street, Merrion Row and the ILAC Centre — you can't miss them.

For slightly upmarket family junkets try the Bad Ass (he's on the billboard) Café in Crown Alley for pizzas and steaks, with wine for the ones who're paying. Great view of passing Saturday crack and a flyover money system. Clery's store in O'Connell Street has a roof-top restaurant, though it's not open-air, alas. Go at a quiet time for a window-seat. If you love good fish and good chips go to Beshoff's in Westmoreland Street — it's dearer than your local but it's very good. Or go vegetarian at the Dublin Resource Centre in Crow Street. The International Food Hall in O'Connell Street has different kinds of fast foods to sample on or off the premises. The Kylemore Cafe on O'Connell Street is good for basic fuel and cakes. The Chicago Pizza Pie Factory beside the St Stephen's Green Shopping Centre and Captain America's in Grafton Street have special deals for under 12s. Eddie Rocket's Diner in South Anne Street looks like it came straight from *Back to the Future*'s Fifties set and a few doors away the Independent Pizza Company is from the same era. What's going on in that street? Gallaghers Boxty House on East Essex Street in Temple Bar has lots on the menu besides the boxty, or potato pancakes, but they're delicious.

Bewley's Oriental Cafés are getting a special entry, because though they have changed in the last few years, they are still part of the nineteenth-century coffee-shop tradition — all dark wood, plush and aromas. There are four in the city centre, in Grafton Street, Mary Street, Westmoreland Street and South Great George's Street. The Grafton Street Bewley's even has its own Museum, high up at the back of the store (or you can go in the oldstyle lift). This was part of the former chocolate factory where you can look at pictures of cream-giving Jersey cows, chocolate-making equipment and work rosters and wages from the early days. Open at 7.30 in the mornings for old-style breakfasts, such as white pudding on toast, Bewleys are probably best known for their luscious buns and cream cakes. They also have home-made vanilla ice-cream. And their tea-caddies make cheap colourful presents, or small treasure chests.

The Powerscourt Townhouse Centre on South William Street has at least nine different eating places (including a pancake place) on the balcony, the basement and the ground floor. They're pretty dear, but if you can get someone else to pay for it, very nice to lounge in and gawk.

MORE FOOD IDEAS

There are numerous Chinese, Kebab and Indian restaurants in Dublin. You could have a look at the raw materials in the Asia Market in Drury Street. The Oriental Emporium at 25 South Great George's Street has lots of packaged treasures like watermelon seeds, fortune cookies and lily bulbs (and lots of other things you can only guess at). If your parents like cooking Chinese bring them something from here — there are so many sauces and they're much cheaper than in ordinary stores. Otherwise most Chinese takeaways will sell you raw bean-sprouts and you can buy spare-ribs in any supermarket, and cook your own Chinese grub.

Bretzels, the Jewish Bakery on Lennox Street, just off South Richmond Street, sells hot bagels on Sunday mornings. These are crusty chewy rolls meant to be eaten with butter and cream cheese. They also have delicious breads and gooey cakes, such as rum balls.

In season, you can pick your own strawberries and apples, and get huge amounts very cheap. You can stuff your face as well as the bags. Watch the papers (and road signs) for the ads. Baldonnel Orchard is one such place. It's an apple and plum orchard, and the Irish Airforce hangs out nearby, so there's free plane-spotting thrown in. Take a right turn at the Roadstone factory on the Naas Road. Strawberries are for the picking in June, in north County Dublin for the most part.

Finally, if you can't afford anything except what's in the home larder, you could try cooking Coddle. Perfect for after a cycling trip, and as Dublin as they come. *You need:*

8 pork sausages
8 thick rashers, or ham pieces
4 large chopped onions or leeks
2 pounds of potatoes, peeled and sliced
2 pints of boiling water
salt and pepper
knob of butter
parsley, if you like it.

Boil the sausages and rashers for five minutes in the water. Remove and keep the water. Put the meat into a casserole with the onions, potatoes and parsley. Season and add enough of the boiled water to cover. Put greaseproof paper on top and leave in a slow oven 200°F or 1/2 gas until everything is cooked. This takes about an hour, but feel with a fork to be sure. Serve hot with parsley and butter. This serves from one to eight persons depending on appetite. (If it doesn't work try a cookery course! See page 133)

Note: For a list of restaurants that specialise in family Sunday lunch, see Chapter 5.

HAIR

Apart from cutting your own hair (and there's a book available on that), shearing can be expensive, especially if you want to keep your hair short. The following hairdressers offer a cheap service if you come as a willing model to their apprentice classes, held mainly in the evenings. You still say exactly what it is you want, but you may not get it, of course (same really as in normal conditions). The cutting will be supervised, however, and it certainly won't be a 'Mother's Cut'. All enquiries were about a wash, cut and blow dry. Prices are all very reasonable.

Peter Mark, 36 Grafton Street. Phone 714399 for appointment.
Herman's Haircare, 81 Grafton Street. Phone 713209.
Robert Chambers, 31 South Anne Street. Phone 771323.
David Marshall Hair Studio, 6 Dawson Street. Phone 777418.
Switzer's Hair Salon, upstairs in Switzer's store. Telephone 773957 for an evening appointment.

These are some of the most well-established hair salons and have a large staff to run the apprentice class scheme. Others may run similar classes on a less formalised basis, so it's worth making enquiries in a place you like. These salons and others sell all the products you need for a daring hair appearance, from gel and mousse to glitter gel and hair make-up. For a simple, short-term colour effect, you can use cooking colouring, sold in any good supermarket or grocery.

JOKE SHOPS

There is a very fine joke shop in South King Street, beside the Gaiety Theatre. It's got a dread display of masks, dog turds, dead rats, spiders, dead hands, as well as 12,000 other things (they say) and farting powder for those special occasions.

In O'Connell Street, on the corner of Cathal Brugha Street, is Funny Biz, another rivetting and ghastly emporium. Here you can get mock wounds, real skeleton make-up and a juke-box-full of cheap jokes and magic tricks.

MARKETS

The Hippo in the Dandelion Market
by Daniel Reardon

A serendipitous hippo,
Content and tubby on the table
Smiled at me in marble.
He was mine for a pound
Which was just about mine.

I milled around the market-place
Wanting his happy fatness
To roll upon my desk.
I clutched the crumpled note
And strode back to the stand.

All the junky jewellery and curios
Sparkled as before, but the hippo
Was gone — sold.
I sank in thin despair
And spent the pound on beer.

Once upon a time there was a wonderful place in Dublin called the Dandelion Market — it was an exciting place to be on Saturdays and Sundays until developers killed it. It sold everything from hippos to blueberry pancakes. But nowadays there's a variety of markets. Mother Redcap's off Francis Street near Christ Church is full of bits and pieces at weekends. You could also take in the Flame on the Hill audio-visual trip to pre-Viking Ireland in St Audoen's Church nearby. The Blackrock Market (Saturdays and Sundays), (See page 114) beside the Garda barracks in Blackrock rambles all over several houses and yards and has gimcrack shops, junk, books, records, toys, clothes, plants, food and a great buzz. The Blackberry Market on Lower Rathmines Road is also a junk market: it's a good place for old radios and appliances.

Then there are the centre city shopping centres, which are really upmarket markets, and very pleasant places to stroll around.

THE ILAC CENTRE has entrances on Henry Street, Moore Street and Parnell Street. It's shaped like a huge cross and in the heart of it is a cool fountain area. At one end there are bubble-lifts that crawl up like lady-birds to the car-park levels. There are two restaurants and plenty of sit-down space, though the centre gets very crowded on Saturdays when lots of people decide to sit around. There's an excellent toyshop, several video and record outlets, good gift shops and lots of clothes shops placed all around the balloon-launch pad, and some of them are mentioned separately here.

The ILAC Centre also has a wonderful library. It's the Central Library of the Corporation libraries and anyone is welcome. The children's library is crammed with really new books, lots of places to sit, a tape tree for listening to stories, and lots of toys for very small kids to play with. There's also lectures and videos for older people in the main library, newspapers, magazines and listening areas for music (classical, folk and jazz). It's a great place for a library and it's well used.

THE POWERSCOURT TOWNHOUSE CENTRE is a place to be taken to by someone with money and a generous heart. It's a hand-some, luxurious market though it mightn't like to be called a market because it's so expensive.

You get to it from Grafton Street by going down the little alley-way called Johnson's Court, or by going in the main entrance on South William Street. These wide steps lead up to Powerscourt House, a beautiful eighteenth-century house, and the shopping centre is out the back, if you like, in the court and stable yard. There are three storeys of galleries overlooking the courtyard, all covered in so you can sit out in all weathers.

The shops are a real mixture. On the ground area there are some cheap-enough stalls, with toys, jewellery and gimmicks. You can buy bonsai trees here too. Don't forget to try the flavoured ice-creams and pancakes on the ground floor too.

ST STEPHEN'S GREEN CENTRE is at that end of Grafton Street. This is a comfortable twentieth-century variation of an old indoor city market. It's always buzzing with action. Three galleries, lots of stairs and escalators and you still might miss the amazing glass clock in the middle! Apart from the dozens of conventional shops there are some little gems here, dealing in crafts and sports (see other categories). On the top floor is a mini-market corner with exotics like conjuring and juggling aids, bonsai, beads, cheap clothes and a clown shop. There's a good ice-cream stall on the bottom floor.

THE SQUARE in Tallaght is a shopping centre with a difference — its pyramidal shape. Inside there's a good mix of shops, stores and restaurants on different levels, but also a radio studio. 2FM broadcast from the Crow's Nest twice or three times a week, and you can hand requests directly into the studio. Above all this again is the UCI 12-cinema complex which runs a Saturday morning club for children — see the papers for what's showing.

MOORE STREET has so far survived all the threats to murder it, and you will probably see why. Once you pass the topmost stalls you can buy the cheapest fruit and vegetables in the country. In summer you can buy buckets of strawberries and raspberries for the family for half nothing. The radio butcher should not be missed for his sheer alive-alive-oh, and sometimes you will see fish, crab, lobster and cods roe on sale in the open, like the old fish shambles.

For the Dublin Corporation **FRUIT AND VEGETABLE MARKET** proper, go down Henry Street, Mary Street and into Little Mary Street. The market is housed in a redbrick Victorian custom-made building, a little like the leopard houses in the Zoo. All round the door

tops you can see carved fruit and animals and inside, mounds and crates of the real thing. Open very early every weekday morning, and you must buy in bulk. By the end of the day there are often bargains to be had — like the sixty-five daffodils I was once given *free*.

Dublin's **BIRD MARKET** is a shadow of what it once was when you could nearly buy an ostrich. It's in an alley off Bride Street, opposite St Patrick's Park, every Sunday morning from about 11.00 am. Canaries and budgies are the main tweeters, but some wild birds like yellow-hammers are for sale here too. Birds used to be common centre-city pets: they took very little room, cost hardly anything to feed, and reminded people of the country they couldn't get out to see.

MODELLING

There are several specialist modelling shops. Modeller's Den in Aston Place just behind Virgin Megastore has remote-controlled aeroplanes and suchlike. Marks Models in Hawkins Street has a vast collection of cars, trains, rolling stock and landscaping, plastic model kits and scientific kits and games. They do train repairs. All Models in Bride Street do cars, boats and planes; there's a model railway shop at 18 Monck Place in Phibsboro, and there's the Model Motor Shop in the Stillorgan Shopping Centre which has cars of all sorts from radio controlled to matchbox.

For model soldier and fantasy game enthusiasts absolutely the best method is to make your own, and the excellent Prince August Moulds in Cork operate a postal service as well as selling their kits through toyshops. You make the lead soldiers in a little frying pan (supplied) and then paint them. Write for a catalogue to: Prince August Moulds, Kilnamartyra, Macroom, Co. Cork, Telephone 026-40222.

MUSIC

Golden Discs (Grafton Arcade, Mary Street, ILAC Centre, Stephen's Green Centre), HMV (Grafton Street and Henry Street) and Virgin Megastore on Aston Quay are all excellent chart and album release outlets. You can find video and game stocks in most of these branches. Claddagh Records in Cecilia Street behind the Central Bank stock Irish and folk music from just about everywhere.

Opus 2, 24 George's Street, have classical and spoken arts. Sounds Around in O'Connell Street and Pat Egan's Sound Cellar in Nassau Street are good for more way-out pop. Always try and have the record number when you're looking for something that's not in the charts. For second-hands and golden oldies try Freebird at 6 Grafton Street. Golden Discs in Grafton Street and the Sound Cellar are also concert ticket stockists. You can make a record of yourself to backing tracks (karaoke-style) at the Centre Stage studio kiosk on the top floor of the Stephen's Green Centre.

You'll get sheet music in Opus 2 in George's Street, Walton's in North Frederick Street and McCullough Pigott in Suffolk Street. The assistants are very helpful. Walton's is a dream emporium for anyone who's lucky enough to be buying any class of musical instrument. Some people go along every weekend and drool over the range of guitars, but there's everything from concertinas to concert harps behind the lovely old facade. McCullough Pigott's have a good selection too, and if you're stocking a full band you could try McCullough Pigott's brass, woodwind and drum floor. Better still, if you fancy yourself on the jazz clarinet or reveilling the neighbourhood on a trumpet, did you know (a) that these woodwind and brass instruments are horrendously expensive and (b) that you can rent one before you decide to buy? A make-up-your-mind-is-this-your-life period of three months rental is operated by Educational Music Services Ltd., 22 Mountjoy Square (742310). It's a very popular scheme. And for anything at all from a triangle to a bagpipes try Goodwin's, the pawnbrokers half-way up Capel Street, or Charles Byrne in Stephen Street. They have an amazing collection, and every instrument must really have a story to tell.

The Dublin Corporation Music Library is in the ILAC Centre library. You pay a low annual fee for your borrower's card and they stock tapes, CDs and vinyl in the following categories: classical, folk, jazz, spoken arts, musicals. You can borrow sheet music too and learn-to-play type books. (Details on how to get involved in music begin on page 126)

ODD SHOPS

Everyone can probably draw up a list that deserve to be seen or patronised. Here's my list.

Read's the cutler's — in Parliament Street. It's actually the oldest shop in Dublin. The cutlers were the sword makers to Dublin Castle, and they still have every kind of knife you can think of. The shop used to face the other way around — it's so old that Parliament Street wasn't there when it was built.

An old-fashioned tobacconist's shop is a good stock house of cheap, presents for your parents. Try Fox's at the end of Grafton Street (it also sells rugby tickets). Amazing pipes and tobacco that fell off a pirate ship, perfumed snuff, or coloured cigarettes (Sobranie's in bright pinks and purples) make good choices, and there are also some lovely wooden boxes.

There is at least one lovely old-fashioned sweet-shop with glass jar displays of real story-book sweets. Go look at Kavanagh's in Aungier Street.

Samuel Greer, saddler and harnessmaker, in Poolbeg Street, behind the Screen Cinema, is a reminder of a horse-filled Dublin. Get your dog's lead here to make a link with the past — it's a lovely shop.

Memoirs in South Anne Street stock mock-Victoriana, tiny toys and Christmas stocking fillers, ceramic miniatures, jewellery and other attractive bits and pieces.

Finally, in the odd shop list, have a look at the most beautiful, most luxurious shop in town. It's Weir's, on the corner of Grafton and Wicklow Streets, a jewellery, glass and china shop. Not so great outside, but inside it's a treat. Huge, with glass cases full of valuables, and massive tickings from massive clocks. You have to hold your breath in case you knock anything over. It's really quite decadent looking, though there are small, reasonably priced things here too if you look.

PARTIES AND CELEBRATIONS

Well, what do you like to do? Home parties with balloons, magic, animals, disco etc, can easily be masterminded by taking a look at the large 'Entertainers' entry in the Golden Pages. Similarly 'Party Planners' gives you a list of people who hire out equipment like bouncing castles, shoe houses, etc.

Getting outside the home: Parties can be arranged in the Zoo — you don't have to be a member. McDonalds do parties in all of their restaurants — by arrangement. Play and adventure centres generally offer a party service with full meal and about an hour of rocketing and bouncing on whatever sliding, climbing and squeegy equipment they have. Some have challenging materials suitable for all ages and sizes up to 13 years, others stay strictly with the smaller ages. Enquire on the telephone: you must book for parties anyway. Most are open seven days a week. Try: Wally Wabbits in the Pye Centre, Dundrum (983470); Giraffes in Coolmine Industrial Estate (8205526) and in Swords (8408749); Injun Falls in Belgard Road in Tallaght (597440); Bambams on Kilmacud Road, Stillorgan (2884529); Captain Venture, The Square, Tallaght (596039); Omni Adventure World, Omni Centre, Santry, (8428844); The Zoo, Leisureplex, Coolock (8485722) and the Fun Factory, Monkstown Road, Dun Laoghaire (2843344). Laser Adventure Games combined with bowling are a big draw and there are two centres that do a deal with a party meal thrown in; Strand Bowl on the North Strand (741868) and Quasar and Dundrum Bowl (980209). Children's farms can arrange parties or provide room for your own party provender. (See pages 97, 98) And the extremely active and tough could try Skirmish, the assault course in Co Wicklow — they cater for parties (2873399 — See page 137). Or you could organise a watery fun party at Fun Tropica in Mosney, bringing a picnic. You'll need transport for all these out of town runs.

PET SHOPS

Pet shops are rare in Dublin, and they don't, quite rightly, keep puppies or kittens. Mice, birds, fish, hamsters, gerbils and all their food and accessories are kept though, and they are interesting places. Tighter controls have been passed so that the trade in large exotic birds and other species is dying out. Uncle George's in Sackville Place, Wackers Pet Shop in Parnell Street and the Dublin Pet Stores in Capel street are good general stores, the Dublin Bird Centre in George's Street Arcade have supplies and cages: occasionally also tarantulas and what look like pet dragons! Jebi's Aquarium in South Richmond Street is also for specialists — it may be the smallest shop in Ireland, but it's got things like celestial telescopes, and sometimes, piranhas. (See more piranhas at the National Aquarium, page 63)

Meanwhile, if you have a sick pet, free treatment is available in the Veterinary College clinic in Shelbourne Road, Ballsbridge. The clinic is open during college terms (the same as school but shorter) and you must get there before 11.00 a.m. Telephone to make sure — 683511. Cats should be brought in baskets or zip-up bags. Your dog won't be able to bite the vet — the College provides muzzles to stop him.

Apart from the listed veterinary surgeons there are several animal clinics that offer treatment at reduced cost. The Blue Cross has a mobile dispensary (tel: 385085 for details). St Francis Dispensary at 163 Church Street, off the quays, operates a clinic three nights a week, Monday, Wednesday and Friday, 7.00 p.m. - 8.30 p.m. DSPCA have clinics in Tallaght, Ballymun and Drumcondra (tel: 772779 for details). The Cat Protection League does trojan work in rescuing sick and stray cats and they will give you any information, or settle you with a new cat pet. They also have a junior section with its own magazine (tel: 908652). (For ways of getting involved with animals see page 144)

PHOTOGRAPHS AND POSTERS

One-hour Photo shops will enlarge and mount your photographs and they can also rescue old photographs that have no negatives. You can visit the Gallery of Photography on Wellington Quay, where there are good exhibitions. They also have posters, cards, books and camera magazines (these last are also available on loan in libraries).

For general posters, either paper, framed or block mounted, try We Frame It in Dawson Street and the ILAC Centre or Athena in the

Stephen's Green Centre. They both have good selections. The UNI-CEF shop in Exchequer Street has posters (cheap), beautiful cards, diaries and calendars that would brighten up the dullest room. The National Gallery, the Municipal Gallery and the IMMA have excellent selections of posters and cards from their own collections and abroad. Cinemas and film distributors will sometimes give away advertising posters, as will travel agencies (especially at holiday fairs) and some embassies. It all depends on the way you ask and the way things are with them.

ROOM DECORATION

There comes a stage when doing up your room (or bit of a room) becomes pretty essential. Here are some ideas for Room Things, ranging from very expensive to zilch. Department stores have all the basics.

Furniture: O'Hagan Design, Capel Street, do cheerful bunks and beds. Pretty Things of the Irish Life Mall, Talbot Street, do beautiful though dear wicker furniture, ranging from rocking chairs to bookshelves and picture frames. Nimble Fingers Toyshop, Stillorgan, have desks and, occasionally tables, small chairs, toy boxes. You can ask about ordering. Orange-boxes for box shelf-making (sand, paint with bright colours and glue together) can be got free or for a few pence. Bring a persuasive person to the Corporation Fruit Market.

Cages/aquaria for fish, gerbils etc.: The Dublin Bird Centre, George's Street Arcade does a good range of both.

Pictures, wall-hangings, kites, fans etc.: (See Photographs and Posters in this section.) Slumbers, 68 Dame Street, specialise in children's bedroom materials. Pretty Things of the Irish Life Mall, In Shops in the ILAC Centre and Stephen's Green Centre have all kinds of small and large ideas. Clowns, china ornaments, rude signs for rooms, tiny bric-à-brac from all over the world, little baskets, dried flowers, large ceramic animals are some of the stock you can hunt for. For kites see Toyshops — kites make great wall decorations.

Large Stuffed Toys: Switzer's of Grafton Street and Arnott's of Henry Street stock the incredibly soft, incredibly realistic stuffed animals that probably cost more than the real thing. See also the Kilkenny Design Centre, Nassau Street for stuffed animals that can be ornaments or furniture.

Plants: Try a bottle or bean garden, or a window box. Quinnsworth Lifestyle in Mary Street often have cheap bottle gardens. A coffee jar will do for a bean garden. Otherwise go to a garden centre with parents. They're cheapest.

SPORTS

Department stores and shopping centre supermarkets usually stock good sports gear and equipment. But for nitty-gritties you need special shops. Here are some city ones.

The Scout Shop in Fownes Street, off Dame Street, will welcome non-scouts also. Camping gear, knives, uniforms, belts, badges are all here. Bramac's in Liffey Street is a really oldfashioned, interesting shop. They stock camping equipment, anoraks, belts, knitted hats, ropes, tartan shirts, warm sweaters — mostly cheaper than anywhere else. Elvery's (who used to have an elephant as their shop sign) of Suffolk Street and the Great Outdoors of Chatham Street, off Grafton Street, are sports palaces. You can buy everything from a snow mobile to full diving gear here, and no one minds you just having a look. The sports clothes though are rather dear in these shops — best bought in a big store.

Sport America, on the top floor of the Stephen's Green Centre, is just what it sounds. Baseball mitts, bats, football togs and great psychedelic surfing and skateboarding gear is stocked.

Fishing afishianados will be fair bait for Rory's Fishing Tackle in Fleet Street.

Horsey people can try Callaghan's saddle-soaped corner in Brown Thomas's department store. There's a life-sized wooden pony that small people enjoy sitting on. Another saddler, and a very nice-looking shop, is Samuel Greer in Poolbeg Street.

STAMPS/COINS

Stamp collectors can go to the Philatelic Office in the GPO for Irish stamps and order first-day issues. The office runs the Voyager club for young people (See page 134). Michael Giffney at 39 Lower Ormond Quay is a specialist dealer who will give advice (370859). And although Stamps, Albums and Accessories at 165 Rathgar Road may not look like a shop, here too you will get much help and encouragement. Mornings only (tel: 972520). Small dingy antique shops and second-hand booksellers often have coins, old stamp albums and old postcards, and there's much to be found at the monthly Collectors' Fair in the Mansion House. It's advertised in the papers.

TOYSHOPS

Toys, like books are sold everywhere, but the special shops are the best. However, don't forget that big supermarkets often have a huge stock of well-known brands cheaper than anywhere else. Quinnsworth is particularly good, and their shop Lifestyle in Mary Street is always worth a visit because it has good, cheap toys. Virgin Megastore on Aston Quay is good on board games, and the latest film and television spin-offs. Paddy Barrett's in Mary Street is probably the best-known toyshop in Dublin — it's got everything, cheap and dear, you can think of. Very good on soft toys and puppets, it's also got electric model kits and radios and watches.

The Early Learning Centre at 3 Henry Street (beside Arnotts) has a huge range of toys for babies and younger children, art materials, musical toys and kits of all kinds.

The Art and Hobby shop was already mentioned: it's at the top of the Stephen's Green Centre and it's especially good for crafty toys and kits. The Dolls Hospital is at 62 South Great George's Street. It's exactly what its name implies — where missing eyes and arms, bald patches, voiceboxes and so on are taken care of whenever possible. Teddies are also treated. But that's not all — it's also a dolls' clothes and a specialist doll's house shop. You can buy Irish-made wooden houses or, better still, get someone nifty to make you one and save your money for the furniture. Everything is to scale — one inch = one foot in our world and you can get things like chandeliers with real bulbs, washing machines that spin, drop-leaf tables, bunks, cots, potties, Welsh dressers and so on. If you think the stuff is magical, which it is, then look at the 'collectors' furniture. This is aimed at adults who collect miniatures — *perfect* ones.

Memoirs at 21 South Anne Street also stocks doll's house furniture, the wooden kind and the ceramic ornamental kind. They even have 'toy' toys (can you imagine a perfect jointed teddy bear 2 centimetres long or 'toy' toy soldiers — can you imagine the price too?) They also have beautiful bits and pieces, tin boxes, wooden villages, puzzles and all kinds of Victorian tiny toys.

Very cheap toys — like presents for small brothers and sisters, or party stuff, can be bought in wonder shops like Hector Grey's in Liffey Street.

The Apollo One Discount Store in Moore Street is an amazing place. Cheap toys yes, but also things like job lots of boot skates, walkie-talkies, tapes, tools, and other treasures.

Nimble Fingers in Stillorgan is obviously not a city shop, but it's got toys and equipment you can't get in other places. Like trampolines and kit bags of building bricks, wooden dolls' houses and miles of bedroom friezes. Plus good baby toys, marbles, paints and some old-fashioned toys.

YOU

I have called this the 'You' entry because it's a list of places to buy things with Yourself on them.

T-shirts: T-shirt Print of the ILAC Centre and Stephen's Green Centre, or Apprentice T-shirt Print of Stephen's Green Centre will print your name or whatever you like on a t-shirt or sweatshirt.

Mugs, plates: Muggins of the Creation Arcade off Grafton Street will paint your name and an animal or toy design of your choice on mugs, plates and cereal bowls. You place an order and it takes a few weeks.

Identity bracelets: Most jewellers engrave bracelets and tags.

Monograms: You can get fancy monograms (initials) done on anything fabric that you cherish by Monographix — a service operating in Brown Thomas, Grafton Street. Tiny or big, price depends. Makes a good present too.

Stationery: Personalised stationery is a luxury. But you could try DIY with...

Rubber Name Stamps: The Rubber Stamp Co., Capel Street. Just walk in and they will do one for you.

Name (or anything you like) Badges, personalised balloons: Balloon Man Party shop in the Stephen's Green Centre carry a range of name balloons. Foto-pop in the same place will print badges and gimmicks for you.

VIDEO AND COMPUTER

You won't find hardware outlets listed here — that really is up to you.
The Virgin Games Shop at 2 Dawson Street has a large range of
computer and hobby games and both they and the Virgin Megastore
on Burgh Quay keep a list of contacts for hobby games clubs and
fantasy clubs. Mr Calculator in Duke Street, despite the name, has a
good selection of games, as does Peat's of Parnell Street. The Acorn
Education Centre in the Grafton Arcade stocks a large selection of
educational software (for Acorns). For mail order educational software write to School Software Ltd., Tait Business Centre, Dominic
Street, Limerick, for a catalogue. They cater for most computer
systems.

Chapter 3

MUSEUMS AND
SOME CREEPY PLACES

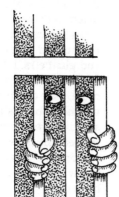

Yes, museums have a dreary, indigestible reputation. They get themselves associated with school projects and wet Sundays and rising parental tempers. Mostly it's their own fault. Until the recent past, very few Irish museums tried to attract young people on a regular basis — with activities, treasure hunts, competitions, special leaflets about their treasures and so on. This is beginning to change in some promising places — with well-presented audio-visual displays, display booklets and tapes for young people and so on. But there's not enough of this yet — sponsors, *please* take note of this very valuable and longlasting way to draw attention to yourselves. Museums really are crammed with treasures, ranging from famous paintings to ferocious weapons, from emperors' robes to ancient dolls' houses, from mummies to friendly ghosts. So I have gone to earth in museums and ferreted about and come back with a list of things to look out for. It's the kind of list I would like to have had before I started, if you follow me. I hope you do. Oh, and the title of the chapter — it's not just museums you'll find in the following pages: there are round towers to climb, castles to invade, jails to break out of ... just remember that Monday usually means CLOSED.

Museum of Natural History. Tel: 618811.
Entrance: Merrion Street, beside the Dáil.
Open: Tues to Sat 10am - 5pm; Sunday 2pm - 5pm. Admission free.

If you belong to a species whose hackles rise at the thought of visiting a museum this one might convert you. It's a fascinating place, a museum that should be in a museum — shaped like a Victorian helter-skelter.

At the very top you are surrounded by exotic leeches and tapeworms and you can look down on suspended skeletons of whales and giant elks. If these don't take your fancy you can view a dodo's remains or a roc's egg or a tarantula eating a humming-bird. Or best of all, stay down to earth with the Irish animals exhibition on the ground floor. It's the best place for learning how to recognise birds and discovering how animals look in their own habitats. Don't miss the beautiful snowy owl, the osprey who is more punk than anything walking the streets, and for an idea of what might be swimming below you in Dublin Bay have a look at the sunfish. Findus, eat your heart out.

National Gallery of Ireland. Tel: 615133.
Entrance: Merrion Street, other side of Dáil.
Open: Monday to Saturday 10.00 am - 6.00 pm; Thursday 10.00 am - 9.00 pm; Sunday 2.00 pm - 5.00 pm. Admission free.

The National Gallery is a place to conquer in parts rather than all at once. If you like pictures that tell a story and are full of characters and adventures, visit the Irish, Flemish and Dutch rooms — Breughel, Vermeer and Steen are great story-painters. There is a science fiction picture from the seventeenth century and faces that you might recognise by Hals, Goya, Rembrandt and El Greco. Anyone who likes fairy tales and romance will love the Burne-Jones princess and the Impressionist room.

The best introduction to the paintings is to attend some of the free lectures or guided tours. The porter's desk has an up-to-date news list of goings-ons. Activities for children follow no regular calendar but when they happen they are excellent. They are advertised in the What's On section of the newspapers. Otherwise you can join the regular guided tours on Sundays at 2.30 pm. Lectures are on Tuesdays, Thursdays and Sundays.

Other services are: *The Library* and *Bookshop*. There is a friendly and beautifully stocked art library downstairs which is open from 10.00 am to 5.15 pm Monday to Friday. You can buy cards and posters from the gallery bookshop — they look great on walls. A *restaurant* with good cakes. A *picture clinic*. If there's a dark oil painting in your attic you can have it identified free of charge at 10.00 am on Thursdays.

The National Museum. Tel: 618811.
Entrance: Kildare Street, beside the Dáil.
Open: Tuesday to Saturday 10.00 am - 5.00 pm; Sunday 2.00 pm - 5.00 pm. Certain rooms are closed during certain hours; groups and interested parties should check beforehand. Admission free.

The National Museum houses all the Celtic treasures you have ever heard of, from the Tara Brooch to the Ardagh Chalice and back again, and anything of historical value you find with your ferret or metal detector should be turned in to them too (if you find anything like the Derrynaflan Hoard you will be very lucky). Gold, silver, pewter, amber and yew-wood were the Celts' favourite materials and their taste passed down into early Christian art — look out for the way artists and craftspeople worked tiny spirally animals into everything. Look out also for Ireland's oldest wheel and a nasty neck chain for prisoners. These are all part of the Treasury exhibition, and to concentrate your mind and eyes, you can watch an excellent audio-visual show before roaming.

The main floor has two exhibitions: Ór — (Gold) which, if you close your peripheral vision and forget that this is a museum, might make you think you had walked into Tiffany's or Cartier's jewel stores. These gold ornaments, beaten thin, twisted or scrolled, are shining bright and perfectly to twentieth-century taste. Many of them are over 4,000 years old, and come from Ireland's great gold rush during the Bronze Age. Think again of panning a river!

The other exhibition is around the walls — the oldest bits of Dublin city life. A Viking's all, from dustbins and pots and pans, to gaming board, dice, puzzle jug, toy boat and graffiti, which were dug up in the Christ Church/Wood Quay area. You might also like the dolls' exhibition on the ground floor beside the historical toilets, or go see the small mummy in the Egyptian room or James Connolly's blood-stained vest in the 1916 room.

There's an excellent museum shop in the lobby.

Heraldic Museum and Genealogical Office. 2 Kildare Street. Tel: 618811.
Entrance: At the Nassau Street end; the handsome redbrick building.
Open: Monday to Friday 10 am - 12.45 pm; 2 pm - 4.30 pm. Admission free.

If you ever wanted to design a personal family crest/motto/seal or whatnot the Heraldic Museum is the place to fill your mind with dragons rampant and severed arms or fleurs-de-lys. It's just one room, with a mixed selection of exhibits; seals, heraldic stamps, family banners, an armoured helm, a herald's tabard like the White Rabbit's from Alice in Wonderland. Not for all tastes, but if you like design and knights at arms you should drop in.

For details of ancestry tracing at the Genealogical Office see the Inside Jobs chapter.

Dublin Civic Museum. Tel: 6794260.
Entrance: South William St, near Powerscourt Townhouse Centre.
Open: Tuesday to Saturday 10.00 am - 6.00 pm: Sunday 11.00 am - 2.00 pm. Admission free.

This little magpie of a museum is peculiarly Dublin. It's lodged in a small eighteenth-century house, which despite its comfortable dolls' house neatness, has always been associated with the public. During the War of Independence the Supreme Court used to meet here in secret.

In the lower hall are panoramic engravings of Dublin which really give a sense of what cabs, coaches, riders, street-sellers, children with hoops etc. looked like en masse. There are old shop signs and a tiny model biscuit factory. Ireland's real giant, Patrick Cotter from Cork, who went on tour, all 8 feet 6 inches of him, is commemorated here by his shoes which would fit a slender-toed elephant.

The museum has regular exhibitions like 'The Emergency', Fire-fighting equipment in Dublin, Model Soldiers, Canal life and Victorian Frogmen. Every Christmas there are treasure hunts for children during the holidays. The Old Dublin Society meets and holds lectures here (visitors welcome) on Wednesday evenings at 8.00 pm, during the winter months.

Dublin Castle. Castle Street, off Dame Street. Tel: 777580.
Entrance: Gates on Castle Street (just left after City Hall).
Open: Monday to Friday 10.00 am - 12.15 pm, 2.00 pm - 5.00 pm;
Saturday and Sunday 2.00 pm - 5.00 pm. Admission free to Castle
yard. Admission fee to State Apartments.

Dublin Castle has a free part and a paying part, and the free part is
the most like a castle. As you enter the gates you will notice there is
no drawbridge or portcullis, although there is a sentry. They *were*
there when the Castle was built in 1204 by King John. But the Castle
was rebuilt in the sixteenth and seventeenth centuries so that the
English Viceroys could live and work here in style. (The style is the
bit you pay to see.)

The Castle has a medieval plan of two courtyards — in the lower
one, over in the right corner, is one of the original towers. This is the
famous tower from which Red Hugh O'Donnell escaped not once but
twice, in the freezing winters of the 1590s. Unfortunately the Black
Tower is not open, but the little Chapel Royal beside it is. It's a tiny
romantic Gothic-style church crying out to be peopled with knights
and damsels, though it was really built in 1807 by Francis Johnston.
His design, apart from being medieval-looking, was very crafty;
although all the work looks as though it is solid masonry, it is in fact
crafted from wood, painted to look like stone. Touch it and see. You
can see why if you go round the back of the chapel, follow the walls
and see the watchtowers on what was the city boundary. Underneath
you the river Poddle is flowing and a solid stone chapel would sink
into it. They did.

During the Great War of 1914–18 the Castle was used as a military
hospital and an attempt was made to capture it during the 1916
Rising. Now it's maintained by the State for the inauguration of a
President, for entertaining foreign heads of state and for European
Community functions. The State Apartments are on view when there
is no State business going on there. They are beautifully maintained
eighteenth-century rooms with stuccoed ceilings and gorgeous chandeliers where balls and receptions took place during the 'Castle'
season — from Christmas to Easter.

Just as you come into the Castle, on your right, was the scene of
one of the Castle's greatest mysteries. It was from here that the Irish
Crown Jewels were stolen in 1907, while under a heavy guard — just
like a Pink Panther film. They've never been found, so away you go.

Bank of Ireland. Tel: 776801. Entrance: College Green portico.
Open: Normal banking hours: Monday to Friday 10 am - 12.30 pm,
1.30 pm - 3 pm. Thursdays, open till 5 pm. Admission free. On
Tuesdays only there is a guided tour of the old parliament by Dublin
historian Eamonn Mac Thomais. Admission is free: go to the House
of Lords at 10.30 am, 11.30 am or 1.45 pm. Groups should make prior
arrangements with the bank's public relations department.

An accident of history turned this vast building into a bank — it was
designed to house the very proud Irish parliament that was largely
responsible for the growth and importance of Dublin in the eighteenth century. And mud streets or no mud streets, the people of
Dublin took a great interest in the doings of parliament, coming into
the galleries to watch, or sometimes to riot.

The architect, Edward Pearce, would have done well for himself
in Hollywood building film-sets because the huge curved walls with
the pillars are a fake. Not that they would fall down if you kick them
— but the building is like a giant thermos, with an inner wall and an
outer wall. Inside it's all much smaller than it seems from without.
The porters will show you the old House of Commons, now the
Banking Hall, which used to be known as 'Goose-pie' because of its
dome. The House of Lords is a beautiful chamber — no traffic noise
can be heard in here — and contains a mace, a chandelier and a
grandfather clock that have outlived all the great speeches and the
corruption of the Act of Union in 1800. Also on display is Maundy
money — tiny coins which were given to the poor on the Thursday
before Easter and could only be used on that day. Ask a porter for
admission.

Trinity College and Long Library. Tel: 772941.
Entrance: Main one in College Green.
College campus open to visitors 7 days a week. Guided tours during
the summer — ask at porters' desk. Fee for tour. Long Room (Library):
entry through bookshop, signposted. Monday to Friday 9.30 am - 4.45
pm; Saturday 9.30 am - 12.45.

Trinity College is a private institution but very beautiful inside and
no one is barred from entering unless they are troublesome, or unless
the Trinity Ball is on and they don't have tickets. Queen Elizabeth I
founded the College in 1592 'to "civilise" the Irish and cure them of
Popery'. It's a residential university and some students are lucky

enough to live in the eighteenth-century quadrangles and have their rooms cleaned for them — a very ancient college custom.

Buildings to look out for are: the Dining Hall — on your left, set back a bit and looking like a miniature Trinity College itself. Eating here is called 'dining in Commons' with High Tables and Low Tables — High Table diners wear gowns. Grace is said in Latin and there's a free glass of Guinness for everyone. You can see them troop in at about 6.00 pm every day. The Rubrics are the tall redbrick block and they're the oldest dwellings left in Dublin — 1700 the date.

The Museum Building beside the 'new' (1967) Library contains lecture rooms and some skeletons. It's a beautiful building designed by Victorian architects Deane and Woodward. Inside it's like a Turkish palace, but stare carefully at the windows. You'll be able to recognise the work of these designers all over the city from the windows alone. (Try Dame Street and Kildare Street for starters.)

The Long Library is where the busloads of tourists head for — it's got the Book of Kells among more modern bestsellers like first editions of Dante and Shakespeare. Even if you think the Book of Kells is taboo to true Dubliners have a look at the library. It's all gleaming lines of shelves, ladders, and books that act as a background for the beautiful carved spiral staircases. Readers used to study at the top of the long ladders, perched like owls or bats in the gloom. And look out for Brian Boru's harp (or at any rate Someone's ancient harp) — it was stolen and held for ransom some years ago.

To celebrate Trinity's 400th birthday a Treasury exhibition centre was built underneath the Long Room. The exhibitions are advertised in the newspapers.

The new Arts Block (easiest entry from Nassau Street) houses the Douglas Hyde Gallery which has good art and photographic exhibitions.

City Hall. Tel: 6796111.
Entrance: Lord Edward Street, facing Parliament Street
Open: Daily 9.15 am - 12.45 pm, 2.15 pm - 4.45 pm. Admission free.

The City Hall was originally the Royal Exchange built in 1769 which thirty years later acted as a torture chamber. Now it's the home of Dublin Corporation and so is the single most useful building in the city, though it's a bit gloomy looking.

The City Archives are here and you can get all sorts of historical information if you have the right questions. You can also get a leaflet on Dublin's coat of arms, with its cheery castles. The treasures from here will presently be shown in a museum, probably the Civic Museum. They include the gigantic City Sword and Mace, which are so big that only a tournament knight could have carried them. The Corporation also owns, along with its fleet of rubbish trucks and acres of swimming pool, a very awesome article — the Ancient and Original Charter of the City of Dublin, dated 1171, with the signature of Henry II and all the Norman nobles.

The Chain Book of Dublin is also a prize possession. It was a kind of medieval Golden Pages that used to be chained to the Tholsel (Danish word for Guildhall) which was opposite Christ Church Cathedral. It is written for the most part in middle English, middle French and Latin but there are early Dublin Corpo gems like the ruling that millers who diddled their customers would be hanged from their own mill beams, or the inventory of all the hideous types of chains and tortures in Newgate prison. There's also a list of brewers — all women.

Marsh's Library. Tel: 543511.
Entrance: St Patrick's Close, beside St Patrick's Cathedral.
Open: Monday, Wednesday, Thursday, Friday 10.30 am - 12.45 pm and 2.00 pm - 5.00 pm; Saturday 10.30 am - 12.30 pm. Admission for children free, adults by donation.

Archbishop Narcissus Marsh built this library in the Close in 1701 which makes it the oldest public library in the country. You cannot borrow from the Archbishop's store of books but you can see what the perfect scholar's library was supposed to look like. It's like a pocket edition of the great library in Trinity College. If all the dark wood panelling and ghost stories were not enough to make a student work he could ask to be locked into one of the special wooden cages at the end of the room.

The ghost is supposed to be that of old Narcissus himself, who is reputed to search through the books at night for a letter that his niece wrote him before she eloped. And if that isn't sad enough, there is an account in the library of 'the accidental death of an elephant by burning in the city of Dublin in 1689'.

Number Twenty-nine — Georgian Townhouse. Entrance: 29 Lower Fitzwilliam Street, Dublin 2. Tel: 765831.
Open: Tuesday to Saturday 10.00 am - 5.00 pm; Sundays 2.00 pm - 5.00 pm. Admission free. Large groups by arrangement.

Eighteenth-century children had it tough: the rich ones were banished to the nursery at the top of the house; the much more numerous poor ones hauled coals and water, brooms and linen to the top of the house and back down five storeys to the basement — that's if they were lucky enough to have a job. You can enter briefly into their lives, and those of the adults around them, in this beautifully restored Georgian townhouse, maintained by the ESB and the National Museum. The house was built in the 1790s by an eighteenth-century real estate king and it cost its first owner £320. The audio-visual show at the beginning of the house tour introduces this lady and her family life; then a guide shows visitors through the tall narrow bathroomless house — two rooms on each of the five storeys. The furnishings are completely in period. Watch especially for the everyday details of heating, lighting and toiletries. The most alive rooms are the kitchen and, of course, the nursery, which has a selection of wonderful dolls' houses, as well as a two-hundred-year-old baby-walker.

Dublin Writers Museum. 18/19 Parnell Square North. Tel: 722077.
Entrance: Beside Findlater's church, opposite Garden of Remembrance.
Open: Monday to Saturday 10.00 am - 5.00 pm; Sundays and Bank Holidays 2.00 pm - 6.00 pm. Admission fee. Free access to bookshop and restaurant. Schools and groups by arrangement.

The Writers Museum is unique in Europe and possibly the world. (And not just because this magnificent house contains another miniature house that you can find...)

The exhibition rooms celebrate a roll-call of great Irish writers, gathering first editions of their books, their writing implements, portraits, letters and other clues to their characters. Like the flying goggles of Oliver Gogarty or the animal-embroidered waistcoat of James Joyce. Upstairs the house itself comes into its own. It's a Georgian townhouse, finished in 1769, but embellished also by its later owners. So the magnificent Gallery of Writers which looks like a wonderful place for a party (and is) has a ceiling and friezed walls unlike any other house in the country. Downstairs again you can go through the annexe, past James Joyce's piano, and upstairs into the exhibition room that houses Tara's Palace.

This doll's palace was built by Irish craftspeople to replace another treasure, Titania's Palace, which was sold, of all places, to Legoland in Denmark. The floors, pictures, fittings and furnishings are tiny and intricate: some ivory pieces were made by French Napoleonic prisoners of war.

Downstairs again are the restaurant and bookshop. There's a good young people's selection — check that they have this book!

Hugh Lane Municipal Gallery of Modern Art. Tel: 741903.
Entrance: Parnell Square North.
Open: Tuesday to Saturday 9.30 am - 6.00 pm, Saturdays 9.30 am - 5.00 pm; Sundays 11.00 am - 5.00 pm. Admission free.

This gallery is a lively place with exhibitions of modern art changing all the time. There could be traffic lights one day, rude shapes the next. Regulars are modern Irish painters, sculptors and stained glass artists, and some very famous French Impressionist paintings — half of Hugh Lane's collection. (The other half is in the Tate Gallery, London — there's a swop every five years. It was discovered that his will was badly drawn up when the poor man sank with the *Lusitania* in 1915.)

The loos in the gallery are lovely, the fireplace upstairs has thirty-six different ship tiles. There is also a very fine restaurant.

National Wax Museum. Granby Row, past Parnell Square West. Tel: 726340.
Open: Monday to Saturday 10 am - 5.30 pm; Sunday 12 - 5.30 pm. Schools by arrangement. Admission fee. Reductions for families and groups.

A Swiss woman called Marie Tussaud started the waxworks craze during the Reign of Terror of the French Revolution. She was made of stern stuff, Madame Tussaud, because she worked on famous heads straight from the guillotine. She's in the lobby to greet you, along with some other friendly figures.

The Museum is divided into sections: the Children's World of Fairytale and Fantasy has all the best-known characters (including some fantastic bits of Giant), a hall of goblins, crazy mirrors and, best for some, a secret Tunnel that leads somewhere if you dare... There's a pageant of Irish historical and cultural figures that's added to all the time: a hall of Megastars, and, with a separate entrance, a Chamber of Horrors which comes hallmarked with gruesomeness. Claustrophobics, *don't* try the tunnel here — though toughies will love it.

All the wax figures are made on the premises by a resident sculptor. Live Irish personalities have a face mask made; others are worked on from photographs and other records. A head can take up to three months' work. Interested art students could enquire about seeing the workroom. Before this Museum opened in 1983, there had not been a waxworks in Dublin since 1916, when the last one burned (very steadily) to the ground.

Chester Beatty Library. Tel: 2692386.
Entrance: at 20 Shrewsbury Road, Donnybrook.
Open: Tues to Fri 10 am - 1 pm, 2 - 5 pm; Sat 2 - 5 pm. Admission free. Guided tours Wednesdays and Saturdays, 2.30 pm. Buses: 6, 7, 7A, 8.

First, none of the splendid mansions on Shrewsbury Road look like libraries. Second, it's really a museum and art gallery rolled into one. If the Book of Kells does not appeal to you you may not want to look at oriental manuscripts either. But if you like books, bindings, brightly coloured and golden illustrations, calligraphy and general whiffs of the Orient, you may be very happy walking around here. If you wake at night wondering what real papyrus and hieroglyphs look like, you'll find those here too. The Chinese and Japanese rooms have the wittiest and most human pictures and there are an emperor's dragon robes to subdue you. Also tiny delicate perfume and snuff bottles guaranteed to make you feel enormous.

Museum of Childhood. Tel: 973223.
Entrance: Basement, 20 Palmerstown Park, Dartry.
Open: Sundays 2 - 5.30 pm. July and August Wednesdays and Sundays 2 - 5.30 pm. Closed October. Admission fee. Buses: 12, 14.

This museum is a treasure house stocked by top-class fairy godparents. The toys go back several centuries and include a small boy's suit of armour, a three-faced doll for every mood, old folk-dolls made from apples (with instructions), a doll's trousseau with tiny corset and bloomers, and streetfuls of antique dolls' houses. These have perfect details like brass beds, porcelain sinks, mangles, prams, typewriters (this last in a house that belonged appropriately enough to the writer Daphne du Maurier). Even the kitchens have tiny cats and mice.

The pride and joy of the museum is Tanya's Crystal Palace which has its own room in the garden. It's modelled on the famous Titania's Palace (built in Ireland and now in Legoland in Copenhagen) and tiny beautiful things that work are set out in the twenty palatial rooms. They have been collected from nurseries all over the world, royal and noble.

Irish Jewish Museum. Tel: 974252 (for information); 534754.
Entrance: 3/4 Walworth Road, off Victoria St, Portobello, Dublin 8.
Open: May to September. Mondays, Wednesdays and Sundays, 10.30 am - 2.30 pm. Other months: Sundays only 10.30 am - 2.30 pm. Special arrangements for schools. Admission by donation. Buses: 14, 15, 16, 19.

The museum incorporates a small local synagogue (no longer used) over the exhibition area. They're housed in two ordinary houses thrown together, and you'll only spot the museum by its longer windows and the Hebrew plaque outside. Part of the Orthodox rules ordained that one had to walk to the synagogue, not drive, so there were several small synagogues around the South Circular Road area, which was the principal Jewish district in Dublin. The exhibition traces the history of Jews in Ireland from 1079 (five arrived and were sent away) through all the different migrations that occurred, usually after persecutions in Europe. It's extremely well done. There's even a tiny twenties kitchen, laid out for Chanukkah, with all the kosher foods involved. There's information on Jewish writers and artists, Jewish schools in Dublin and the youth organisations. The most famous twentieth-century novel in English has as its hero a Dublin Jew, Leopold Bloom, in James Joyce's *Ulysses* (its other hero is Dublin itself). He's here too. It's full of stories, this museum, and the synagogue is full of presences.

Kilmainham Gaol. Tel: 535984. Entrance: Inchicore Road.
Open: June to September 11.00 am - 6.00 pm every day. October to May 2.00 pm - 6.00 pm Wednesdays, Sundays and Bank Holidays. Guided tours. Admission charge. Buses: 21, 78, 79.

The dank chill of Kilmainham's enormous historic walls will have entered into your soul by the time you have edged along its narrow passages, trodden on its wire cage netting and walked over the Fenian dead under the flagstones in the prisoners' yards. Ireland's political and social history from the 1790s to the Civil War in 1922 breathes here through every stone, and sounds to every footfall and clang. And if the atmosphere itself wasn't enough, the museum section in the galleried section of the prison has the artefacts to prove it. There's an introductory audio-visual display in what used to be the prison chapel and then a guide leads visitors through the cell corridors and the execution yards, filling in the heartless background to prison life. Although the Gaol became particularly notorious after the leaders of the 1916 Rising were executed in the stonecutters' yard, debtors, transportees and famine victims also had their tragic tales told here (a child of 8 was sentenced to 5 months hard labour in 1839 for stealing a cloak). There are fascinating document kits available here for both primary and secondary school students. The gun-running boat *Asgard* is in final dry dock in one of the yards.

St Enda's/The Pearse Museum. Tel: 934208.
Entrance: on Grange Road, Rathfarnham (16 bus terminus).
Open: May to August, daily 10 am - 12.30 pm, 2 pm - 6 pm; March, April, September, October, 10 am - 12.30 pm, 2 pm - 5.30 pm; February, November, 10 am - 12.30 pm, 2 pm - 4.30 pm; January, December, 10 am - 12.30 pm, 2 pm - 3.30 pm. Admission free. Buses: 16, 47B.

The Hermitage is a famous museum in Leningrad — it's also a third name for this museum. St Enda's was the school founded by Patrick Pearse for Irish Catholic boys. Pearse called other schools of the day 'murder machines' — he had a point. Belonging to his school was a bit like being in the ancient Fianna. You can see the dormitory, study and some of Pearse's letters and writings.

There is also a nature walk, with booklet available, in St Enda's Park, and there are a lot of curious red squirrels in the trees. There is a small nature study centre for schools as well. Information on it is obtainable from the Office of Public Works, 51 St Stephen's Green, Dublin 2 (613111). By the way, look at the shape of the garden — it's like a Celtic Cross.

The Joyce Museum, Sandycove. Tel: 2809265.
Entrance: It's the Martello Tower, down by the Forty-foot swimming place.
Open: May to September, Monday to Saturday 10.00 am - 5.00 pm. (closed 1.00 pm - 2.00 pm). Sundays and Bank Holidays 2.00 pm - 6.00 pm. Out of season by appointment only. (2806984) Admission charge. Bus: 8; DART.

The Joyce Museum is in a martello tower on the seafront in Sandycove where the writer James Joyce lived in 1904. Inside there are letters and manuscripts, some of his very stylish clothes, and his guitar. But even if you are not particularly interested in Joyce's personal effects, it is a chance to get inside a martello tower and see what it was like to live in one. These stone Rolos were built as watch-towers in case Napoleon decided to drop in — some have since been converted into private homes. (See Beaches, page 116) You can see the round rooms inside this one and climb right up onto the battlements where James Joyce used to shave.

The National Maritime Museum of Ireland. Tel: 2800969.
Entrance: The Mariners' Church, Haigh Terrace, Dun Laoghaire.
Open: May to September, daily, except Mondays, 2.30 pm - 5.30 pm. October, Saturdays, Sundays, Bank Holiday 2.30 pm - 5.30 pm. Schools and groups outside these times by arrangement. Admission fee. Buses: 7A, 8; DART.

The Museum is in a converted mariners' church which is down a narrow street. To get to it just turn left off George's Street after the Dun Laoghaire Shopping Centre. There are so many things to drool over that the retired Chief Petty Officer who sometimes shows young people around often has to impose some naval discipline!

There are two things that you cannot miss — the giant lens from the Baily Lighthouse and the longboat. The lens is beautiful, rotating like the eye of a god with 2 million candlewatts reflecting in its mirrors. The longboat is possibly the oldest surviving ship's boat in the world. It came ashore in Bantry Bay with the French invasion fleet in 1796 and is painted in its original French revolutionary tricolours. There are dozens of ships' models — both steam and full rigged sailing ships, logs, compasses, 'sin bins', a scale model of an oil rig, charts, telescopes and even a nail from the mutinous *Bounty*.

Drimnagh Castle, Long Mile Road, Crumlin. Tel: 2802203 for info.
Entrance: Through the grounds of the Christian Brothers school.
Open: April to mid-October Wednesday, Saturday, Sunday 2.00 pm - 5.00 pm. Other times for schools and groups by arrangement. Admission fee. Buses: 56A (or 50, 55 to Crumlin village only).

This is a very likeable Norman castle that's not much larger than an average semi-detached house. However it probably slept thirty or more people, as well as horses, hounds, cats and other less welcome four-footed creatures. The moat sports ducks rather than fearsome pike but there's an ancillary burglar-alarm in the shape of a 'murder-hole' leading into the undercroft, or medieval store and kitchens. Upstairs the Great Hall (living-room cum bedroom to us) has been lovingly restored in tiles and oak by craftspeople, who fittingly have their heads carved into the roofspace, like any medieval workers worth their salt. Outside there's a seventeenth-century knot garden and some exotic fowl. A guidebook with activities for children is in preparation.

National Aquarium, Bray. Tel: 2864688.
Entrance: halfway down Bray Promenade, on the seaward side.
Open: Every day 10.00 am - 6.00 pm. Admission charge. Groups by arrangement. Bus: 45; DART.

Bray cats have not been told, but 10,000 live fish (and sundry marine creatures) exercise their swim bladders, flex tentacles and generally hang out in this large functional building full of corridors and strange Escherian angles. As with the Natural History Museum, absolutely the best, and most popular, exhibits are the native varieties, many supplied from lobster pots by local fishermen. Slate blue conger eels with elegant profiles show off their length while spotted dogfish reveal both their sharkiness and their mammalian-like eyes at close quarters. ('Real' sharks are promised at time of going to press.) The football-sized octopus sleep a lot and rather appealingly, while rock-pools as you've never seen them can be inspected from underneath the surface. The otherwise lazy ling lay 28 million eggs. Spotting the plaice in the sand is a keen test of observation, but none could accuse the exotics of trying for camouflage. They're arranged according to continent, so you should check beforehand if you're not sure where piranha hail from. There's a sweet shop, and, yes, a keen pet and fish shop on the premises. Fish mania could grow from a visit here...

Castletown House, Celbridge, Co Kildare. Tel: 6288252.
Entrance: from Celbridge Main Street.
Open: April to September, Monday to Friday 10 am - 6 pm; Saturday 11 am - 6 pm; Sunday and Bank Holidays 2 pm - 6 pm. In October hours as above except closing time is 5 pm. November to March, Sundays and Bank Holidays 2 pm - 5 pm. Admission charge. Reduced family and group rates (groups by arrangement) Buses: 67, 76A.

Castletown House is enormous but once it belonged to an average-sized family, the Conollys. William or 'Pa' Conolly was Speaker of the Irish House of Commons: he rose from obscurity to become the richest man of his time in Ireland. His perfect house was built to show this and was begun in 1722. Two architects were involved: one, an Italian, Galilei (yes, that name), the other was Edward Pearce of Bank of Ireland (Irish Parliament) fame. Palladian is the name for this style of winged, pillared house.

You'll see plenty inside. Cracked mirrors in the dining-room, said to have happened when the devil was discovered tucking in. (The devil seems to have liked this part of Dublin, and the Conollys in particular, as he turned up in the Hellfire Club in the Dublin mountains, also built by Speaker Conolly.) There's a Print Room, which is an early and genteel forerunner of the habit of sticking posters and stickers on walls: ladies applied their favourite works to the walls. Visitors to the Conolly household were entertained in a number of drawing rooms, but the favourite was the Long Gallery, an enormous and beautiful mirrored room that the family used much as Norman barons used their Great Halls. In different parts of the house are odd treasures like a sedan chair, carved cabinets with hundreds of secret drawers, a crocodile (yes!), a rat school (yes!), strange and wonderful hat-boxes. Downstairs are the cavernous kitchens (snack bar attached); upstairs there's a fine view of the Castletown Folly, two miles off. It's 140 feet high and it was paved with good intentions — to give famine relief in 1739.

Russborough House, Blessington, Co Wicklow. Tel: 045-65239.
Entrance: to the right past Blessington on the Donard Road.
Open: from Easter to end October, on Sundays and Bank Holidays, 10.30 am - 5.30 pm. Every day in June, July and August. Admission charge. Bus: 65 to Donard.

Russborough was 250 years old in 1991, and was built for a rich brewer called Joseph Leeson (yes, the street, too). He spared no expense, hiring the best of Italian plasterworkers for the interiors, after using the design of possibly the busiest and most expensive architect in Ireland, Richard Cassels. Everything in the house is polished and perfect, and, like nowhere else, there is an air of utter luxury in the rooms you are guided through. Every piece of porcelain, every strand of carpet looks like it was intended to be here from the day it was made. The collection of Old Masters does nothing to take away from this impression — it was built up by the uncle of the house's owner, Sir Alfred Beit. Unfortunately there have been some notorious art robberies from Russborough (some paintings have yet to be recovered) and in 1987 Sir Alfred donated the most valuable pictures of his collection to the State, at the National Gallery. Some priceless pictures from the collection return during the summer for display.

There is a shop and a fine restaurant. The house faces the lake, all greys and greens. Out of sight, and growing apace, is a new development for stately homes in Ireland — a maze. Planted with fast-growing beech, within a fairly short time the maze will be open to puzzle visitors and torture toddlers. Be there with your ball of string!

Howth Transport Museum, Howth Castle grounds. Tel: 8480831 / 8475623.
Entrance: to the right, just before the Castle.
Open: Easter to end September 10 am - 6 pm. Sundays 2 pm - 6 pm. Rest of the year: weekends 2 - 6 pm. Admission fee. Bus: 31; DART.

You get an old tram ticket on entry here. If you loved Richard Scarry books as a small child, or just generally like having large recognisable chunks of the past to stroke, the Transport Museum is a wonderful place. Here, in a gigantic shed belonging to this old Gothic castle, are housed ancient tractors, mineral water trucks, gorgeous old double-deckers and fire-trucks, and the pride of the collection — the Hill of Howth tram, which is being lovingly restored. All the workers are voluntary, and are delighted to talk about their beloved charges, and their plans for them.

The Irish Museum of Modern Art (IMMA), at the Royal Hospital, Kilmainham. Tel: 718666.
Entrance: follow the signs from St John's Rd, beside Heuston station.
Open: Tuesday to Saturday 10 am - 5.30 pm; Sunday 12 - 5.30 pm. Admission free but special exhibitions have a charge. Buses: 21, 78, 79, 51.

This is an art gallery but it's also a historic building (see below). The old soldiers who retired here would be amazed to walk the long bright corridors and peer into their former bedrooms to see what the late twentieth-century contents are. Ever since the IMMA opened in 1991 people have been arguing about the brightness and especially about the glass staircase that ascends to the exhibition area. What do *you* think? Works of Irish and world artists are on view here, with many prestigious exhibitions visiting. You will certainly find plenty to admire. Downstairs is a community project display area and a superb art bookshop where, although many of the books are fabulously expensive, there are great postcards and small gift ideas. There's a restaurant across the quadrangle in the basement of the Hospital.

Royal Hospital, Kilmainham Tel: 718666. (Follow the signs from St John's Road, alongside Heuston railway station.)
Guided tours: Sundays 12.00 pm - 5.00 pm. Admission fee. Restaurant open daily.

The Royal Hospital is the nearest thing Dublin has to Paris and the palaces of Versailles. The Duke of Ormond, who also had the great idea of the Phoenix Park, saw the new home for King Louis XIV's old and wounded soldiers, Les Invalides, and decided that King Charles's soldiers should be just as well served. So, this beautiful, classical, square hospital was built and finished in 1684. The soldiers lived in little rooms, two to a bed, and wore a blue uniform. For exercise, there were the formal gardens, and for a long walk, a trip down to Bully's Acre, the oldest known graveyard in the city. The soldiers had little rooms in the upper storeys. But the architect, Sir William Robinson, saved his genius for the Dining Hall, the Chapel and the Master's rooms, now all beautifully restored. Oak trees from Scandinavia provided the panelling, and sheer genius (or madness) provided the Chapel's ceiling. If you want to know what 'baroque' means don't look in a dictionary, come and look at the Chapel instead. You'll know instantly. The building cost £23,000 three hundred years ago: it cost £20,000,000 to restore it. You can have snacks or Sunday lunch in the basement restaurant — try to figure out how the clock facing the quadrangle works.

St Doulagh's Church.
Entrance: on the Malahide Road, near Kinsealy.
Open: May to September; Sunday 3 - 5 pm. Admission free. Bus: 42.

If God made Wendy churches this is one. Everything is pint-sized in this thirteenth-century church which is nearly perfectly preserved. Perhaps the monk who wrote the Irish poem 'Pangur Bán' about his white cat lived here because the building has a sense of humour about it. From the road you see the myriad tiny windows set at angles where nothing except a toe has any business to be. Inside miniature crooked staircases lead round and up into the tiny, boxy rooms, one on top of the other. There are stone seats and cubby-holes and the hairy watercress grows in all the windows.

St Doulagh was an anchorite. That, for ghouls, is a monk who chose to be walled up in a cell for the rest of his life and fed by his trusted fellows through a cubbyhole. There is also a leper window here so that the unfortunates could attend Mass without meeting squeaky-clean people. Outside in the grounds is the holy well and baptistry; it's so old that St Patrick is said to have happened along to oversee the work.

The Casino, Marino. Tel: 331618 or 613111 (Office of Public Works, for info). Entrance: Signposted (and visible) from the Malahide Road. Open: June to September, daily 10 am - 6.30 pm. Rest of year. Saturdays and Sundays 2 pm - 4.30, or tours by special arrangement. Admission charge. Buses: 24, 42.

Don't come expecting fruit machines. Casino really means 'little house' and that's what the first Earl of Charlemont commissioned his genius friend and architect Sir William Chambers to make, in 1762. What it does have in common with the other kind of casino is trickery. This 'little house' has three storeys, a secret window, Grecian urns for chimney pots, and, of course, a secret tunnel. The excellent guides will tell you about the pineapples that once grew here (the plasterwork shows spades and rakes as well as fancy Greek gods), about the spiteful spoiling of the view, why green paint was more expensive than yellow and about the four friendly stone lions with Tipperary smiles. The original good goods in small parcels. And beautiful restoration work — would make anyone want to be an architect.

Newbridge House, Donabate. Tel: 8436534.
Entrance: Right-turn for Donabate from the Dublin/Belfast road, after Swords; signposted.
Open: April to October, Tuesday to Friday 10 am - 5 pm (closed 1 - 2 pm); Saturdays 11 am - 6 pm; Sundays and Bank holidays 2 - 6 pm. November to March, Saturdays, Sundays and Bank holidays 2 - 5 pm. Admission charge. Reductions for families and groups. Bus: 33B; train from Connolly to Donabate.

Newbridge House, its traditional farm and its parkland (see Parks chapter, page 96) is over 250 years old, and a national treasure. The family who gave Newbridge to the public, the Cobbes, still have a flat in the huge house that was begun by their great (multiply by n times) relative, Archbishop Charles Cobbe. There are plenty of admirable eighteenth-century rooms, but two great ones. There's a private museum, the only one of its kind left in these islands. It's the equivalent of a holiday video or after-dinner chat. Here you can see giant scarab beetles, moths of revolting mien, python skins, a hookah, wheat from a Roman camp, an egg laid by an ostrich in Dundalk (?) and great stuff from the bottom of the ocean, dredged by the science ship *Challenger*. The kitchen is the other great room. It really is a dream kitchen.

You can take a separate tour of Newbridge Traditional Farm, through the beautiful cobbled courtyard. With your ticket comes a leaflet explaining the layout. Round the yard are the dairy, forge, tack room, carpenters' workshop, and, incredibly, the Lord Chancellor's Coach, golden and beautifully sprung (check for pumpkin seeds!), and some other magnificent horsedrawn vehicles. From the courtyard you go through to the farmyard, via the hatcheries — check for eggs cracking. Remember — this is a Big House farm that bore no similarity to the average sized farm of the time, but this farmyard somehow looks like farmyards from every folk and fairy tale. There's a small but noisy collection of birds and beasts — gigantic hens and cocks with feathery breeches; a sow, human-friendly sheep, goats and miniature ponies. There's a killing shed — not in use. You pass by the duckpond and the vinery to the paddocks where there's a small herd of traditional cattle. Back through the walled orchard and garden to the courtyard where you can call in at the coffee bar.

Malahide Castle and Demesne. Tel: 8450940/8452337. (Separate entries for Fry Model Railway Exhibition and Castle Gardens) Entrance: on Malahide Road, just before the village.
Demesne open during park hours (See Parks chapter). Castle open Monday to Friday 10 am - 5 pm (all year); November to March 2 - 5 pm on Saturdays, Sundays and Bank Holidays. April to October, Saturday 11 am - 6 pm; Sunday and Holidays 2 - 6 pm. Admission charge. Bus: 42.

Talbot Street is the city bus terminus for the Malahide bus, and the Talbot family owned Malahide Castle from 1185 until the 1970s. Now the 268 acres belong to Dublin County Council and you can visit without an RSVP all year round. There is great rolling parkland, some of which has been turned into tennis courts and pitches, but most of it can still be raced and tumbled upon. Behind the car park closest to the Castle is a fine adventure playground hewn of wood.

You can do a tour of the Castle inside. From outside it's a mixture of styles, mainly Loch Ness movie, and it has a very small door for its size. Inside, the rooms have been turned into a walkaround museum of Irish furniture — from a medieval banqueting hall to a Victorian nursery. Portraits of faces from history books hang everywhere—the Castle has also become the national portrait gallery. Upstairs there's a gentleman's, a lady's and a child's bedroom, just like the Three Bears. Try spotting the different period styles in the castle by watching details like window shapes, rooms sizes, ceilings and colours.

There is a special children's audio tape available as well as press-on commentary in all the rooms. Downstairs there's an excellent snack bar.

Fry Model Railway Exhibition, at Malahide Castle. Tel: 8452758. Entrance: beside Castle.
Open: April to October, Monday to Thursday 10 am - 5 pm (closed 1 pm - 2 pm); Saturday 11 am - 6 pm (closed 1 pm - 2 pm); Sunday and Bank Holidays 2 pm - 6 pm. November to March, Saturday, Sunday, Holidays 2 pm - 5 pm. Admission fee.

The Fry collection is the Crown Jewels of Irish model railway layouts. It was built up by an engineer, Cyril Fry, during the 1920s and 30s and it's now beautifully housed and maintained in Malahide. There are all kinds of full-size railway mementos on display in the waiting-room, but save your admiration for the tiny and perfect railway systems inside. You'll find the DART going to Howth where the Howth Tramway snakes up the Hill, the famous West Clare Railway and other narrow gauges, Belfast and Cork railway stations, as well as miniature replicas of familiar bits of Dublin like the Poolbeg power station. Anyone who's interested in crafts will love the tiny throwaway details.

The Steam Museum, Straffan, Co Kildare. Tel: 6288412.
Entrance: Dublin/Naas by-pass, turn right for Straffan village. Take right turn at the Straffan Inn; the Museum is about half a mile on the right in the grounds of Lodge Park House.
Open: June, July, August; every day 11.30 am - 5.30 pm. Sundays and Bank Holidays all year round; 11.30 am - 5.30 pm. Admission charge (varying as to whether the visit is on a live steam day or not). School groups by prior arrangement.

Here be dragons — steam dragons, heroes of the Industrial Revolution that changed the life of the world for ever. Now these industrial engines and perfect working models of locomotives and Victorian plumbing systems are dinosaurs, but they can still puff their hearts out though many are creeping up on two hundred years of age. The

Museum is located in a beautifully restored Gothic-style church. The Power Hall contains five fantastic engines, taken from brewery, distillery, factory and ship, and on a working day, the combined power presents an awesome sight. The Engineers Hall has the dwarves: models created for a purpose (but there must have been pleasure too) by the great Men of Steam. Included is Richard Trevithick's (the First M of S) Third Model of 1797 — the oldest of its kind in the world. The train locomotives are quite perfect, each one distinct as no modern vehicle is. There's a portrait gallery of Steam persons and a souvenir shop of Steam artefacts. More mundane steam happenings occur in the tearoom, and at certain times the walled garden is open to visitors. (For more steam activities see page 134.)

The Guinness Hopstore, Crane Street, Dublin 8. Tel: 536710.
Entrance: Signposted off James's Street.
Open: Monday to Friday 10.00 am - 4.00 pm.

The Hopstore (hops, malt, barley, yeast and water are what Guinness is made of) is an art gallery and a museum and today it is an enormous, stunning building. What it was like crammed with hops is anybody's guess. You'll hear that this is the site where the Emperor of Morocco's son was kidnapped but once Arthur Guinness set his heart on brewing dark porter that was it for non-Guinness stories. He fought with the Dublin City fathers for his own water supply to come to him through hollow elm trunk pipes — then he built up his huge empire of gallons. You can walk through the old brewery equipment, and sit through an entertaining audio-visual show, before going downstairs to look at the transport models and into the big bar where adults get a free sample fresh from the brewery and others a soft drink. Upstairs, the galleries usually carry exhibitions worth visiting.

Swords Castle, Main Street, Swords.
Buses: 33, 41.

Castles changed their comforts over the centuries, and so, if they're still used they have a curious mixture of styles, like Malahide Castle or Dublin Castle. Swords Castle however remained stubborn and medieval. This is probably why the owners moved out and it is now a ruin. It was built to contain all the townspeople, their dogs and cats and chattels in times of marauding Danes. However, there are watchtowers, a chapel, stairs, and the battlements are still in excellent shape.

If you'd like to know more there's a local history exhibition in the old library on Main Street, open on Sunday afternoons.

Round Towers (Clondalkin, Lusk and Swords).
Entrances: see individual entries — but always high up. Admission free. Contact Office of Public Works (613111).

Round Towers are the Irish answer to the Great Pyramids and who knows what puzzlement they are causing in far-flung galaxies. Dublin has three very well preserved round towers, two of which can be entered. The towers are at Clondalkin, Lusk and Swords, and they are not hard to find!

Probably everyone except extra-terrestrials knows that round towers were built by monastic communities to protect themselves and their valuables from Viking invasions from the ninth century onwards. That is why the doors are set so far up — when all the monks, plus manuscripts and cats, were inside, up came the ladder. But the doorway is a piece of cake — wait until you open the door and see what lengths they went to to escape the fury of the Northmen. Naturally they could not use a staircase inside in case the outside door failed and the enemy got within — so they had more ladders connecting the various floors which could also be pulled up. The Vikings' answer to all this was (sometimes) to throw in a lighted match and that was that.

You can go up the towers at Clondalkin and Lusk but this guide cannot give it the personal seal of approval since she would have faced a thousand Vikings instead. Apparently it's perfectly safe but you do need a torch.

Clondalkin Round Tower
Key from Mr Henry Burns, 41 St John's Wood, Clondalkin. Bus: 51.
Dates from 776 and was plundered by the 'Horned Ones' in 832. It's
still almost perfect.

Lusk Round Tower
The tower is open from mid-June to mid-September from 9.30 am to
6.00 pm, and there is a small local museum beside it, with the same
hours. In winter the key may be had from Mrs Pat Kelly, Autoview,
Dublin Road, Lusk.

Swords Round Tower
No access. Buses: 33, 41.
Brian Boru's body spent the night here after the battle of Clontarf, on
its way to Armagh.

NOTE

From Dublin's Millennium Year of 1988 until 1991 a huge attrac-
tion in the city was the Irish Life Viking Adventure Centre in the
crypt of St Audoen's Church, just inside the medieval walls.
Emerging from a 1000-year timewarp, visitors were greeted by a
Viking lord of Dublin who escorted them through the smelly
streets, houses and work-shops populated by Norsefolk and their
Irish slaves, who were not slow to poke fun at twentieth-century
clothing and carry-on. At the time of writing the Centre is closed,
but its franchise has passed to the good offices of Bord Fáilte, who
plan to open it again, further downriver, in 1993. Check with them
about developments — the Viking Adventure was a saga you
could take part in.

Chapter 4
MEDIEVAL DUBLIN

PLACES TO VISIT...

1. Cook Street medieval gate to the city. Walk up the steps to St Audoen's Church.

2. Christ Church Cathedral (b.1172, perhaps earlier). Look out for Strongbow's tomb. Boy pretender king crowned here in 1487. (Mummified cat in crypt.)

3. Dublin Castle, with its Black Tower.

4. St. Patrick's Cathedral (b.1192). The Poddle used to flood the cathedral and Patrick St. Now it is all underground. Look out for the stone from St. Patrick's Well. Listen for choirboys at Evensong; they go to school across the road.

5. This is the site of the very oldest part of Dublin — the Ford of the Hurdles.

6. St. Michan's Church. Go to the crypt and look at the leathery hand of the Crusader. There are preserved bodies here. Mon – Fri: 10a.m.– 12·45 and 2p.m – 4·45. Sat: 10a.m. – 12·45. (Open on Wednesdays, June to September.)

7. St. Mary's Chapter House, Meetinghouse Lane. (Mornings only, in winter.)

   This has a 6-foot drop and very musty old air inside. Here is where Silken Thomas threw his sword on the table and started a rebellion. (He was executed in 1537.)

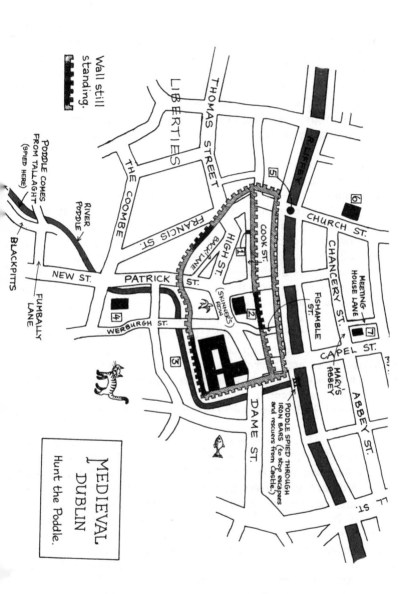

MEDIEVAL DUBLIN
Hunt the Poddle.

Wall still standing.

Poddle comes from Tallaght (spied here)

BLACKPITTS

FUMBALLY LANE

RIVER PODDLE

NEW ST.

THE COOMBE

FRANCIS ST.

THOMAS STREET

LIBERTIES

PATRICK ST.

WERBURGH ST.

4

3

BACK LANE

HIGH ST.

(SKINNERS) ROW

1

2

COOK ST.

DAME ST.

5

R. LIFFEY

CHURCH ST.

6

Poddle spied through iron bars (to stop escapes and rescuers from Castle.)

CHANCERY ST.

FISHAMBLE ST.

MEETING HOUSE LANE

7

CAPEL ST.

MARY'S ABBEY

ABBEY ST.

ST.

Dublin is very, very old — but you need to be a bit of a detective to find out the way it looked 200 years ago, not to mention 900 years ago or before that again. The map over the page shows the size of medieval Dublin, which was, of course, a walled city: at every street entrance there was a gate. There was an inner wall too, and that is there still at Cook Street. Dublin was this size in 1200 AD — when it started to grow the 'suburbs' were called 'Liberties' and were attached to the guardianship of certain saints. And then it grew more... and more...

Even though it's hard to pick out the medieval features without a lot of poring over books, some things will give this part of Dublin away for what it is. The hills, for one. Nowhere else in modern Dublin city are there found these up-and-down streets. The first settlers, and then the Danes, built the city to be nice and safe on top of the hill. The narrow winding streets are another giveaway — though some of their colourful names like Cutpurse Lane and Hangman's (Hammond) Lane have gone. But Fishamble Street is still there: it was the ancient fish market, just up from the river. Another giveaway is the drop you have to make when you enter any of the medieval buildings marked on the map. Ground level goes up about one foot every century.

A visit to the Flame on the Hill audio-visual presentation in St Audoen's church on High Street will help to give the flavour of pre-Viking times and afterwards. It's an unusual place for a show — watch for the giant clam water fonts from the South Seas and the cloistered restaurant. In summer the shows are on the hour between 10 am and 5 pm: telephone 791855 to check other times. Admission fee.

Medieval Dublin was noisy, busy, dark inside dwellings (no windows, rush candles), and very smelly. People did their washing and took their drinking water, not from the Liffey, but from a river called the Poddle. Can you see it on the map? It was their lifeline, even though it sometimes overflowed and flooded their houses beyond repair. Now the Poddle has been driven underground and most Dubliners never think about it. But you can use this map to go on a Poddle hunt, because the Poddle actually surfaces in the grounds of a convent in Blackpitts. You can also see where it flows into the Liffey — if you cross over to Ormond Quay. You could go further and find some old maps of Dublin and trace the Poddle right out to where its source is, in Tallaght/Walkinstown. It's above ground quite a bit after

Harold's Cross. But meanwhile, when you walk over these ancient streets, remember that they are built on water.

If you want to learn more about the buildings on the map, and about medieval Dublin, you must read other guide-books and histories. There is a short list at the back of this book, and your library very likely has project files on old Dublin. The National Museum, and the promised Wood Quay Museum (if it's built) will fill in a lot of homely details for you. But the ground work calls for mystery-solving qualities.

Chapter 5

I-SPY SUNDAY WALK/
SUNDAY LUNCH

ER..
UM....
MAYBE...
OR...

An I-Spy Sunday Walk — in the late morning when the oddest things can be happening — for younger readers and their parents. The walk goes all the way from Findlater's Church in Parnell Square to St Patrick's Cathedral (it *is* a Sunday!) but you can start or stop anywhere along the way. Check your map to help plot your route.

Findlater's Church looks over the Garden of Remembrance, an angular park for sitting about in. The church cost only £20,000 to build and it had its top removed recently like a piece of Lego, to be smartened up.

Do you spy the vast chimney stack above the Candy Store opposite? Try to count all the pots. Now think of all the fireplaces that had to be lit and cleaned by housemaids and swept by chimney-sweep boys. Just beside it is Walton's music shop which is worth a peep through the windows. (See page 40)

Walk down the hill. You are now in O'Connell Street. It is perfectly straight and 150 feet wide. How many trees? (65). The trees were famous for their starling cities — thousands of starlings used to nest here and raise their babies — but probably the level of lead pollution got too high for them because now they've moved.

You may have been born in the Rotunda Hospital in Parnell Street on your right. It was the first mother and baby hospital in the whole world, built in 1757. Its very suitable name came from the nice round building, most recently a cinema, that curves around the corner.

Do you see the taximen's altar a bit down O'Connell St?

On the right hand side of O'Connell Street is an upmarket pool hall, Ned Kelly's. This game goes back a long way — in the second century an Irish king called Conn Cetchathach left to his heirs 'fifty-five billiard balls of brass with the pools and cues of the same materials'.

The 'floozie in the jacuzzi' is the cheeky name given to the fountain with the long-tressed green person enjoying the splashing water. She's not a mermaid, she's Anna Livia, the spirit of the river Liffey, and she was created in Dublin's Millennium year of 1988.

Beside the Café Kylemore on your left you'll see the Happy Ring House, the most loved neon sign in Dublin (along with Why Go Bald on South Great George's Street).

You might spy the religious lady — though she's more likely to be around in the evenings. She preaches in the dead centre — An Lár — the traffic island where there was once a climb-up monument called Nelson's Pillar. Dublin doesn't have an actual 'Speaker's Corner' like the one in Hyde Park in London but the G.P.O., especially at weekends, has rallies, usually political ones. This is mainly because it's the centre of the city and partly because the G.P.O. was the scene of the Proclamation of Independence in 1916.

You can go into the G.P.O. every day of the week. The row of telephone boxes has recently been revamped and it's usually full of people making long-distance calls to everywhere possible. The bronze statue of Cuchulainn makes an excellent hiding place. Do you see the raven?

Eason's store is closed but if you don't know it, go there on a weekday. It's a book store, stationers, toys, health food, record shop on four floors and was voted the single most interesting shop in Dublin by thirteen-year-olds in Sandymount High School.

Across the road down Abbey Street are the *Independent* offices. If you want to, go down and look at the press photographs and old newspaper printing press in the *Independent's* window and you'll also find, set into the pavement outside, the first of the Leopold Bloom sculptures. There's a trail of fourteen, marking a route taken by Mr. Bloom, the hero of James Joyce's novel *Ulysses*, from the *Independent* office (only then it was the *Freeman's Journal* office) up to the National Library in Kildare Street. The sculpture trail was laid down during Dublin's Millennium year of 1988. It's off our beaten track — but *you* could walk it another day, over O'Connell Bridge, Westmoreland Street, College Green, Grafton Street, Nassau Street, Duke Street,

Dawson Street, Molesworth Street, ending in Kildare Street. See if you can spot all 14 — maybe with a little assistance from Bord Fáilte or Dublin Corporation. You'd be walking into the greatest novel of the century!

Do you see the temperature check flashing?

Next stretch of O'Connell Street is the place to stop for a milk shake or burger or a quick blast of invader games. Either side of the road will do — there are many outlets trying to get you in.

The last monument in the street is Daniel O'Connell's own — the street was known as Sackville Street until 1882 when it was officially renamed. The angels are not angels but Victories. Can you spot the one with a bullet hole in an uncomfortable place? They are excellent viewing stations during parades.

You are now on O'Connell Bridge. If you look towards the sea, how many bridges do you see? In old photographs, masted ships came right up to this bridge because it was the last Liffey Bridge. If you walk onto the little traffic island at the junction of D'Olier Street and Westmoreland Street (the fork facing you) you'll find one of the most attractive 'statues' in Dublin. They're footprints — all shapes and sizes, with toes and without — try them for size!

Turn right and go up the Liffey on the north side. There used to be a lot of auction rooms here and you'll soon find one to peek at all the strange things out of other people's old houses.

The Pierrot Club is a jazzy place, once an auction room. (Not for younger folk.) But if you fancy a smaller version of one of those sad-faced pierrot dolls, look at the gift shops in the ILAC Centre or the Powerscourt Centre.

The Liffey is soupy and green. Sometimes mullet can be seen swimming in shoals — in summer anyway. Do you see anything interesting floating by? (For more mullet see the National Aquarium, page 63)

The Ha'penny Bridge is the curved footbridge over the river. It's a lovely old bridge that turns up in every film ever made about Dublin. Story is that there used to be a halfpenny toll for pedestrians crossing. But before you tread its boards have a look at the Dublin Woollen Company on your right. Outside it is another friendly sculpture, two women shoppers, sitting down, bags beside them, having a chat. When the statue was first erected some viciously witty vandal stole one of their handbags.

Go through Merchant's Arch and up the pretty lane; you're in the Temple Bar area, one of the very few parts of the city that has a medieval-type street pattern. Narrow pathways with attractive small shops, restaurants and galleries line the mainly cobbled streets. In 1991 a film called *Far and Away* was made here, starring Tom Cruise — the whole area become nineteenth-century Boston for a few weeks. You can certainly stop for a snack here if you haven't already done so.

Do a wiggle round the Central Bank building and into Dame Street. Dame Street is wide and old and used to lead (a) up into the old walled city of Dublin or (b) down to the grand eighteenth-century parliament (the big Bank of Ireland). If you can, imagine coaches belting down here; you'd have to hop to get out of their way and, if female, keep your skirt lifted out of the muck.

Keep right. Do you see the masks and make-up in Bourke's theatrical costumiers? You can buy clown make-up kits in here and all sorts of fancy dress can be hired. Do you see the Stage door of the Olympia Theatre — the one the actors use? See where the road dips a little? That's because the underground river, the Poddle, is right underneath.

Go past the City Hall and left into Castle Street.

Turn into Bride Street. Do you feel the hill going down? That's why old Dublin was built here — safe on top of a hill.

Ahead of you is St Patrick's Cathedral and park. It's very tumbledown on your left-hand side but stay on that side because sooner or later you come to Peter Street. Turn in and you will see (it starts about 11.30 am every Sunday) the Dublin Bird Market: it's very tiny now — it used be a grand affair with every sort of hookery, like sparrows painted all colours to pass as exotic birds. (See page 39)

Have a whirl round the park or into the Cathedral. Then if you come up Stephen Street, via Bride Street, this leads you into George's Street, Wicklow Street and Grafton Street, where you can treat yourself after a busy Sunday walk.

SUNDAY LUNCH

Sunday is the day most families pick for their outings and picnics — there's too much to be done on Saturdays. If you decide to splurge and eat out, great, but do a little bit of planning because (a) lots of eating places take a rest on Sunday, and (b) it can be enormously expensive. McDonald's in O'Connell Street and Grafton Street are prime spots for Sunday lunch but here is a short list of restaurants and hotels that also cater for Sunday family lunch, and actually welcome children. It's a small selection chosen either for the kind of family fare offered, and/or because of an interesting location. Moving out of the city centre restaurants, it's always advisable to book a table for Sunday lunch and you (or, more properly, whoever is paying) can make enquiries about prices and menu then. All of the choices below are low to middle range in price. All offer either a separate children's menu or half-portions of the standard menu.

CITY CENTRE

Judge Roy Bean's Tex-Mex Restaurant, 45 Nassau Street, 2 (6797593) Mexican or Irish brunch, burgers.
Bad Ass Café, Crown Alley, Temple Bar (712596) Pizzas, burgers.
Captain America's, Grafton Court, Grafton Street (715266) burgers, Mexican.
Chicago Pizza Pie Factory, Stephen's Green Centre (781233) pizzas plus.
Flanagans, 61 Upper O'Connell Street, near Henry Street (731388) burgers and pizzas.
Gallagher's Boxty House, 20 Temple Bar (772762) Irish specials and international.
National Gallery Restaurant, Merrion Street (615133) Sunday lunch 2 - 4 pm. European dishes, half-portions available.

IMMA, Royal Hospital Kilmainham, near Heuston Station (718666) 12.30 - 3 pm. Roasts, fish, vegetarian, half-portions available.
Hugh Lane Gallery of Modern Art, Parnell Square (788238) 12.00 - 3.00 p.m. Roasts, half-portions available.

HEADING SOUTH

Step Inn, Stepaside, Co Dublin (2956202) Carvery.
Blakes, Stillorgan village (2887678) Carvery, burgers.
The Brasserie, Monkstown Crescent (2805174) European.
Dalkey Island Hotel, Coliemore Road, Dalkey (850377) Roasts, fish.
Kilternan Golf and Country Club, Kilternan (2955559) Carvery, fish.
Marley Park Hotel, Grange Road, Rathfarnham (946908) Roasts, fish, vegetarian.
Captain America's West, Dun Laoghaire Centre (2808119) Burgers plus.
Hunter's Hotel and Garden, Rathnew, Co. Wicklow (0404-40106) Roasts, fish.

HEADING NORTH

Garden Café, The Zoo (713450) from 1.00 p.m. Varied, from sausages to roasts.
Portmarnock Country Club Hotel, Strand Road (8460611) Carvery.
St Lawrence Hotel, Harbour Road, Howth (322643) Roasts, fish.
Le Chateau, Main Street, Swords (8406353) European, roasts.
Silver Lining Restaurant, Airport (372439) Varied.
Saddlers Restaurant, The White House, The Ward (347511) Roasts, fish.
Grand Hotel, Malahide (8450633) Two sittings at 12.30 and 2. Varied.
Brahms and Liszt, Swords Road (after airport) (8428383) Roasts, fish, pasta.

NOTE
If you would like to do a walking tour with the help of experts, there
are several organised guides. Dublin Footsteps is one such ~~
who do historical and literary trails during the
children can go free with one adult ticket. Telepho.
Bord Fáilte (747733) for details.

Chapter 6

PARKS, GARDENS AND FARMS

This chapter heads for the great outdoors — the outdoors that were made especially for city slickers — parks. Dublin is lucky in the number of parks it has, and I have not covered even half of them here. Let's face it, some parks are as ugly as sin, but they can still be favourites because you are used to them. Here I'm taking a look at some of Dublin's oldest parks and at some farms you can visit. So if your local is not here, don't be insulted. You can tell me about it for the next edition, and meanwhile try visiting some of the others on the list.

Northside parks first!

Phoenix Park
Buses 10, 14, 38, 39.

The easiest way to 'the Park' is to walk, bus or cycle up the quays to Parkgate Street with the Wellington Monument (duke not boot) as your Pole Star.

The park is huge (1,752 acres, enclosed) and walking from one end to the other is no laughing matter, but it is worth getting to know the various corners, and also where it gets its name. There is a lovely statue of a phoenix bird in the centre park but he is really there under false pretences. If anything he should be an albatross because the name 'phoenix' comes from the Irish 'fionn uisce', clear water, refering to a spring still to be seen in the grounds of the zoo.

Phoenix Park was turned into a Park in 1662 by James, Duke of ond. He wanted a royal deer-park, presumably in case Charles

II ever turned up on the doorstep looking for some crack, but from the start the deer-park was taken over by Dubliners.

The main road through to Castleknock takes you past the sports grounds and the turning for the Zoo. More about that later. This main road is lined with old Dublin gas-lamps which are still in working order. As you go upwards towards the Castleknock Gate, look out for all manner of strange sportsmen, especially on Sundays. Horse-riding is commonplace, but walking races are good to look at and my favourite is bicycle polo on Sunday mornings at 11.00 am. Real horse polo is played in its own grounds on the right, on three afternoons a week: Wednesday, Saturday, Sunday, May to September. It's free to watch and a very skilled, old-style, sport it is. You might also see or at least hear the buzz of model aeroplanes flying.

More ordinary sports are played here also. On your left you pass a huge area called the Fifteen Acres (multiply it by thirteen to get its actual size). Because this area is so wide open, it was the perfect place for a million plus people to gather in September 1979 to hear Pope John Paul II say Mass. It was a colossal spectacle.

The deer should not be missed. They are usually found in the spinneys near the Castleknock Gate. These deer are the dappled, fallow variety and the young ones are quite tame, but watch your dog if you have one with you. Although the deer are not native, they have been here since Charles II's time and so they deserve a bit of respect. The Office of Public Works keeps their number secret but you could try counting them. The other Irish deer, the native red deer, are becoming very rare throughout the country. Red squirrels are also less common than they used to be, so if you do see any make or class of squirrel, it's more likely to be a grey one.

At the Knockmaroon Gate in the extreme south-west of the Park is an Information Centre with info on the park's wildlife and nature trails. Just beside it is an easily followed Nature Trail which heads down deep into the Furry Glen. Good for a family afternoon.

On the main road through to Castleknock you will also see the white houses: Aras an Uachtaráin on your right and the American Ambassador's residence on your left. Near the Castleknock Gate, o your left in a hollow, is the Ordnance Survey. The OS is respon not just for plotting every needle in every haystack in every townland in every barony in every county in Ireland, but also, in the early days of the OS, intrepic tury gentlemen collected songs and folklore, put top towers and dug castles out of manure heaps, all in the name of the OS, and built up in fact a large part of Irish history that would have been lost forever. If you are an interested and fairly advanced geography student, you may be able to make an appointment here — otherwise it's private.

Poised at the top of the Hollow is the excellent Phoenix Park Tearooms, restored from Edwardian days and serving cakes, snacks, and, in summer, strawberries and cream.

And now for coming back. If you return by the back of Aras an Uachtaráin — which was formerly the home of the Viceroys to Ireland, and where President Robinson now lives — you are doing what last century's Dubliners often did, hoping to get a gawk at the Lord Lieutenant and his entourage. Coming back round towards the Park Gate, you find the People's Park where bands used to play and nannies used to try to keep their charges from rolling down the Hollow. Today the same nannies could make their task much easier by going into the great little Adventure Playground just inside the gates of the Park. Across the way, large Dublin Metropolitan Policemen used to march smartly up and down in the barracks yard — it is now the Dublin headquarters of the Garda Siochána.

This edition was published before Ashtown Castle, in the Phoenix Park, was opened to the public, but by the time it reaches your hands you will be able to go right into this medieval keep, built most likely by Norman Crusaders. Later it became the home of the British Under Secretary, whoever that should be, one of whose perks was as much venison as he could eat, from the herd.

As well as the restored castle building, the Office of Public Works have built an interpretative centre on the site, which celebrates the history — and it's a colourful one — of the Phoenix Park itself. There will be an audio-visual presentation, and going back through the park, visitors should see quite a few things they missed on the way in. For details of opening hours etc, telephone 613111.

The Zoological Gardens

Phoenix Park. Buses: 10, 14. Tel. 771425. Admission charge.

If someone in the family takes out family membership for a year, everyone gets in free as often as you like to go; you can also have special lunches, and you get copies of the ZooMatters newsletter. Admission to Fota Wildlife Park in Cork is also included.

I KNEW I SHOULDN'T HAVE EATEN SPAGHETTI FOR TEA.

Feelings run high about the keeping of large wild animals in captivity and there is controversy about city zoos all over the world. You may prefer to visit a free-range park like Fota in Cork. What you see in Dublin Zoo is the layout of a Victorian garden park enclosure. But the Zoo has certainly come a long way since it was founded in 1830 when the only beast on show was a solitary wild boar. Now there is always young stock from successful breeding programmes, and always something new. There have been famous visitors on loan like pandas and koalas.

A recent construction is the bat house which you visit in the dark: the large Rodrigues bats, an endangered species in the wild, are to take up roost in Dublin's bat house. The lake birds are beautiful and the sealions full of watery high spirits. Monkeys and snow leopards have new enclosures and breed very successfully — you might see a baby monkey tucking into fruit sandwiches. There is a Pets' Corner where children (and adults) can get right up to and pet gentler beasts, especially the small cuddly ones like kids and fawns — not forgetting the resident Labrador. There are mouse cities and stick insect cities and other non-threatening collections. And did you know that the MGM lion, who snarls at the beginning of the movies, is a Dublin Zoo lion?

Meanwhile, if you're broke, you can see many of the animals by walking round the outside of the enclosure! Wolves, big cats and sealions are some of the easily spotted inhabitants (the leopards are *not* easily spotted!).

The Botanic Gardens, Glasnevin
Buses: 13, 19, 19A. Tel. 377596

On somewhat the same lines as the Zoo, except that it's ⌐ inhabitants do not move, are the Botanic Gardens. If ever hit Ireland, this will be their headquarters. Mea dens are run by the Department of Agriculture who the Royal Dublin Society who got them from a poetic politician called Tickell in 1795.

The summer is the best time for visiting. The plan inside the gate will tell you where everything is, even Thomas Moore's Last Rose of Summer. The herb garden is a delicate and delicious, nose-educating spot, and nearby is the poisonous garden. For sheer, unbearable jungle heat, see how Tarzan you can be in the tall conservatory: missionaries and intending travellers to Venus could be tested here. Tall enough for the huge Amazonian creepers, the building itself is a lovely piece of Victorian glass construction. Don't miss the lily pond; it's a terrific spot for frog-spotting.

The river Tolka forms one of the Garden's boundaries; it slides past but right in the garden it becomes a water-lily pond. If you sit here very quietly on a warm May afternoon, you are likely to see the most enormous dragonflies, like model helicopters, blue and whirring. There are red squirrels here too. You will see lots of young gardeners — the Department runs a degree course in horticulture here, supplying all the parks' gardeners and many private nursery gardeners. You can ask for advice yourself — if you have a digging bug, it's a good place to go.

Also in Glasnevin is a cemetery (the main entrance is on Finglas Road), a very large and a very famous one. There's a mock round tower built in 1869 as a monument to Daniel O'Connell. He is buried here and so is Charles Stewart Parnell; but, even more to the point, it's the most traditional Dublin burial place. Street-sellers sell flowers outside the gates at weekends — they're not allowed inside. But the caretakers have an easier job nowadays; in Victorian times they were kept up half the night on the watch for body-snatchers who took rings and other valuables and then sold the bodies to medical students.

St Anne's Park, Raheny.
Buses: 30, 44A.

It's called St Anne's because there was a holy well of that name near the sea road part of the park. Dublin girls used to have a prayer for the busy saint: 'Dear St Anne, send me a man, as fast as you can'.

The park used to belong to the Guinness family, and when the Corporation first took it over just before the 1939-45 war, the area was used for growing wartime vegetable rations. Now it's the biggest public park after the Phoenix Park, stretching from Raheny to Clontarf. You'll find forty football pitches and eighteen hard tennis courts without tripping over your feet. You'll find the huge and glorious rose garden by the smell and there's a clock tower made of flowers which is neat in every sense.

Apart from the flower gardens, it is not a formally laid out park so there is a lot of room to move around, to roller skate, fly kites and model planes, do cartwheels or just go for a ramble and explore. Sometimes there are free open-air concerts. Just remember — dogs like flower beds for different reasons than human beings, and rose gardeners can be thorny people.

However, you can join in the Choose Your Rose Competition which is held every year on a Sunday in July. If you prove to be a good judge you could win a prize. It may be the nearest you get to bloodstock judging! (For further details, contact Dublin Corporation at St Anne's, Telephone 331941.)

St Stephen's Green, Grafton Street.
Open until sundown, whenever it is, all year round.
Buses: You can walk! Routes from O'Connell Street, Westmoreland Street, Grafton Street.

Dubliners call this park simply Stephen's Green. In one form or another, the Green (another name for it) has been around for a long time. When Dublin was a walled city, it was a common grazing ground where citizens could 'walk and take the open aire'. But, as ever, the Corporation needed more money so, in 1663, they offered the Green to the well-off burghers and big-wigs to stake their claims. They could build houses or not, as they wished, around the Green and if they did, the house had to have two storeys and a basement. There was a wall around the Green itself with a ditch, and every householder had to plant six healthy sycamore trees near this ditch. Whether this was to keep the citizens out or in is not certain. At any rate the Green grew up fast and was claimed by Dubliners, just like the Phoenix Park.

Nowadays the Green is famous for its pond with its ducks and geese, for sunbathing, for statues and for free lunchtime music in the summer. The pond is fed with water from the Grand Canal at Portobello and it's a very strange sight to see it being cleared annually. One half at a time gets drained and looks like a mud swamp while bewildered ducks try to figure out what's happening. Mallard and greylag geese are the common water-birds here and you may be lucky enough to see all the traffic stop while the famous ducks who hatch their eggs on Leinster House lawn bring the offspring up to take the waters in the Green. Early June is the usual time.

There are ten statues in the Green — see if you can find them all — including a modern memorial to W. B. Yeats by Henry Moore with holes in it. (There is another Moore sculpture in the Front Square of Trinity.) There is also an adventure playground hidden in the Green and an unusual plot, a garden for the blind — the names of the plants are written in braille on tags and the plants may be felt all over for texture and shape.

There's a crazy bye-law in the Green which says you cannot even wheel a bicycle through so watch out for sticky wardens.

Merrion Square
Buses: 7A, 8, 45 and, if there are no buses, you can walk. Route: Westmoreland Street, College Green, Nassau Street, Clare Street. Open till sundown.

Merrion Square has been transformed from a square into a park. (Fitzwilliam Square nearby is still a square — only the residents of the square have keys and the privilege of disporting themselves inside the railings. See page 57 for entry to a square house.) The Catholic Church owned the green square and had plans for building a cathedral on it. That would make three and a half cathedrals in

Dublin. But in 1974 the Square was handed over to Dublin Corporation — lock, stock and barrel.

Merrion Square is now yours — and you can survey the three Square sides of Georgian houses as if you owned one of them. The gardens are beautifully landscaped, there's a small playground and interesting sculptures lurking in all parts of the square. Lots of open-air events happen here in summer time, and it's a perfect place for a city picnic.

Herbert Park
Buses: 7A, 8, 10, 45, 46A.

A perfect park. It's a case of double parking because the park is cloven down the middle by an avenue.

On the Ballsbridge side you can watch bowling (very sedate) or play tennis (very cheap).

The Donnybrook side of the park has everything else — pond, swings, an Edwardian drinking-fountain, bandstands, Brothers Grimm-type shelters, playing fields, hidden levels and corners, and it reaches right over to the river Dodder.

The park had its summer of glory when King Edward VII opened the Great Exhibition here. It looked like a cross between the Arabian nights and a willow-pattern tea set: there were sunny pavilions everywhere and the pond had boats and a water-chute, with little bridges crossing over the bottlenecks. There was even a Somali village and tribe packed into the grounds and when a Trinity student kidnapped a Somali baby the visitors terrified the Donnybrook residents by threatening war.

UCD Grounds, Belfield.
Buses: 10, 11, 46A from Trinity College.

The university grounds are officially private but at weekends the university is unofficially glad to welcome people like you and me. There are many sports pitches and a most luxurious sports complex which is open to non-students in summer for a fee — badminton, squash, gymnasium, table tennis etc.

It's a pleasantly laid out grounds with little spinneys and shrubberies for examination. More unusual is the great fire-pond in the heart of the university buildings. Every weekend modellers bring radio-controlled boats here and have races, wars, embarkations and even ice-breaking, it's rumoured. Sundays at noon you'll find miniature Formula One racing in the carpark near the campus church.

Killiney Hill / Dalkey Hill

59 bus from outside Dun Laoghaire railway station to Killiney (ask to be let off near gate to Killiney Hill). DART

Killiney and Dalkey Hills are big rambly places with parklands, woods, huge rocks, bracken and gorse undergrowth and, of course, some of the best views in Dublin. You can go for a leisurely walk around the summits of the two hills for about 4 miles, gazing at the view. Or else you can plunge into the undergrowth and hide and then creep up and ambush people. Be sure to wear thick clothing if you're going to do the latter. You can watch people hang-gliding off the top of Killiney Hill on a Sunday afternoon if it's windy, and you can watch people rock-climbing in the old quarries on the side of Dalkey Hill in any weather (see Joining In chapter).

The obelisk at the top of Killiney Hill has a plaque which reads: 'Last year being hard with the poor, the walks around these hills, and this was erected by John Mapas, June, 1742'. John Mapas also built Killiney Castle which looks more like a French chateau from the hill. He did a good job on the paths — there is one right around Killiney Hill and another right around Dalkey Hill, and the two join to make a figure of eight. There are a couple of paths leading down to the Vico

Road and the owners of Killiney Castle used to walk over to catch the train into Dublin. (For the beach see page 117)

In case you're wondering, the Wishing Stone on the top of Killiney Hill was built in 1852, why, nobody knows but if you walk around each level from base to top and stand facing Dalkey Island and make a wish, it's bound to come true.

Marley Grange, Rathfarnham
Bus: 47B from Hawkins Street.

This is a huge open park with acres of mown grass and some woodland. It is perfect for frisbees, gymnastic displays, or kites. The courtyard of old Marley House has been turned into a craft centre and you can see potters, antique clock repairers, harp makers, weavers, stained glass makers, silversmiths, goldsmiths, coppersmiths, acoustic guitar makers, at work. There is also a craft shop where you can buy the handcrafts and have coffee or tea and buns. The shop is open Mondays to Saturdays, 11.00 am - 5.30 pm and Sundays 2 pm - 5.30 pm.

It also has Dublin's first public adventure playground, a BMX trackway, and, in summer, a model railway which gives under-tens a real Orient Express-type ride. The playground is quite a walk, about half a mile from the entrance, diagonally, to your right across the large field. But it's really worth it. It looks a little like a Red Indian camp — everything is of wood, made to take assault: a wobble bridge, a fortress with slide-down pole, a tower with rope for swinging, tunnels, and lots of milder but similar stuff for small kids. Across from the playground (no dogs) is the BMX course — you are required to have safety gear. On your way over you pass the miniature railway. In summer, on Saturday afternoons from 3.00 pm to 5.00 pm, the model railwaymen run their steam trains on real coal and it's entirely free. There's always a queue but it moves fast. (For more steam see the steam museum, page 70)

If you have walked round all the parks listed in this chapter and still haven't had enough, Marley Park has just the thing for you. There is a twenty-mile walk through forest and heather, all the way to Enniskerry and Roundwood. It is called the Wicklow Way and is the first stage of a planned footpath the whole way around Ireland. You can get a copy of the route and instructions for the walk from Dublin Tourism at 14 Upper O'Connell Street. Telephone 747733. Alternatively take OS Map sheet 16 of Kildare and Wicklow and study the route on show in the carpark in Marley. The route is signposted all the way so you can't go far wrong. Bring warm clothing, stout shoes, food and drink.

The experts say you average only 2 miles per hour in hilly terrain, so the walk to Enniskerry will probably take the whole day. You can break here and catch the bus (44) back to town or stay in the youth hostel at Knockree near Enniskerry and carry on to Roundwood the next day.

Memorial Park, Inchicore/Islandbridge.
Buses include 79, 65, 21.

Right now this is one of the most extraordinary places in Dublin, and it is potentially, perhaps, the most beautiful park of all. Its proper name is the Irish National War Memorial Park and it was laid out in 1938 in remembrance of the 49,000 Irishmen who died in the First World War. The architect was the very famous Sir Edwin Lutyens, who created dream buildings all over the world. Here in a hollow, surrounded by avenues of trees, is a deserted Roman-like vision of huge fountains and towers, which used to contain book rooms with all the dead soldiers' names. Ahead is a lovely stretch of the Liffey where all the boat clubs practise. Until 1986 wild horses used to wander through the park — they were traditionally grazed on the bank of the river. But the Office of Public Works has restored the park to its former and formal beauty, with thousands of roses and lilies, and water playing. It's a quiet park, very different and well worth rambling in and exploring.

Powerscourt Gardens, Enniskerry. Telephone 2863546.
Admission charges to Gardens and Waterfall.
Open March to October 9.30 am - 5.30 pm. Bus: 44 then $1/2$ mile walk.

Powerscourt is near Enniskerry. The house is a shell, a very beautiful shell, having been burnt down a few years ago. This time it is the gardens you should see. These are landscaped gardens, the kind that are found in only a few stately homes. Gardens like these needed as many servants as the house itself. There is a tiny Japanese garden with bridges and waterfalls, rose walks, shrubberies, a lake, rather algaed now, and walled-in vegetable gardens. Keep a special eye out for the animal cemetery with interesting tombstones like the one of the faithful Jersey cow.

There is also an adventure playground set beside an avenue of huge evergreens. You can buy plants in the garden centre; they could hardly come from a better place and make great presents or room decorations.

You could also visit Powerscourt Waterfall further up the road, it's Ireland's highest. It's good for picnics but go there after a wet spell to get the full effect. Be careful — people have been killed right here.

Fern Hill Gardens. Tel: 2956000
Enniskerry Road — just up from Lamb's Cross. Bus: 44 from Hawkins Street. Open March to November, Tuesday to Saturday, 11 am - 5 pm; Sunday 2 - 6 pm. Admission charge.

Fern Hill Gardens belong to the Walker family who are said to be garden geniuses. They have grown a beautiful place with everything from great redwoods to a laurel maze, from a huge rockery to an old-fashioned vegetable garden, from a stream with secret picnic places to wild ground and a lookout rock. It's a wonderful place most times of the year and if you're entranced with gardening there's a very good nursery which sells unusual plants. You could build a very good herb garden with stock from Fern Hill and have fresh herbs outside your kitchen window.

Malahide Castle Garden. Tel: 8452655
Bus: 42 from Talbot Street.

You might never get to see the actual gardens because the huge park is so well worth exploring. Even when it's full of Sunday families there are hidden corners, playing fields, tennis courts and acres of velvety grass with not one forbidden inch marked out. Very small children go into ecstasies at the sight of all this grass. Perfect for a social kind of picnic, but make sure to clean up because the park is so well kept and so welcoming. It's also free.

The gardens are behind the Castle — you go through a small lodge to reach them. Open 2.00 pm - 4.30 pm May to June. Admission fee for adults, children under 12 are free. Once inside two things that must be seen are the giant thistles, about eight feet tall and straight from a science fiction story, and the oak tree. It's an amazing thing with branches taller than itself and looks as petrified as its Latin name (*quercus petrae*) sounds. Though it's not actually petrified, it's just a sessile oak, grown ancient and hoary. In other parts of the gardens the shrubbery with many narrow grass paths through it makes a good hiding area. But keep to the paths — they're not there for nothing. Another plus for small persons is the grassy slope that would once have been the moat — superb rolling can be practised.

In the rest of Malahide grounds you could search for Yourell's Well or the Lime Kiln, using the free leaflet provided from the Castle admission desk. (For the Fry Model Railway, see page 70.)

Newbridge Demesne, Donabate. Tel: 8436534.
Bus: 33B, train from Connolly.

The park belongs to Newbridge House which you visit along with the traditional farm (See page 68). But wandering through the park itself is free, and it's unbeatable for an outdoor party — you could take the train for a treat. A river runs through, there's a castle inside the gate, meadows, woodland, a secret pond (be careful) and acres of space to hang out.

Massey Woods, Killakee.
Entrance: over the wall, opposite Killakee House Restaurant, on the Killakee Road, Rathfarnham.

Despite the 'over the wall' bit these woods are open to the public, and they're included here, from all the different woods that clothe the Dublin mountains, (a) because they're close, and (b) because they are real mixed woodland, not just Christmas tree woods. There's a little river running through the rocky valley which can be followed by path or by water, pools, falls, glades for picnics, and, throughout, great beeches, oaks and other trees you can try to identify.

The Shackleton Garden, Clonsilla. Tel: 8212216.
Entrance: 1 mile from Clonsilla village, on the Lucan Road. Train from Connolly - Maynooth. Buses: 80, 39C
Open: March to October. First Saturday and Sunday of the month. 2 - 6 pm; also some other Sundays (check by phone). Admission charge.

The Shackleton Garden is a great walled Victorian garden, a type that, were it not for all the visitors, would conjure up *The Secret Garden*. Adult garden-lovers will ooh and aah at the landscaping and the stock, but there's plenty for younger people to find in this large square with all kinds of plant and watery bases — it's not unlike taking part in a life-sized board game. During the summer there are planned activities and competitions for young people, using the grounds outside (check beforehand for details). There's a tea-room and some of the produce of the garden is for sale.

Reynoldstown Animal Farm, Naul, Co. Dublin. Tel: 8412615.
Entrance: Dublin/Belfast Road, turn left for Naul at the Balrothery Inn, come to T-junction and take left, farm is signposted.
Open: Mid March to end of October. 12.00 pm - 5.00 pm every day.
Admission charge. School tours by arrangement. Birthday parties can be organised.

Chickens, goslings, miniature ponies, goats, sheep, rabbits, cattle, donkeys — and large packs of small terriers — are the chief inhabitants of Animal Farm, a working farm. Most of them can be handled, though the more exotic fowl are kept in wire runs. There's a stable-yard, paddocks, a river walk, a tearoom, and a key available to open up the megalithic passage grave at Fourknox, two miles distant. A great weekend outing.

Straffan Butterfly Farm, Straffan, Co. Kildare. Tel: 6271109.
Entrance: Dublin/Naas bypass; turn right for Straffan, left at T-junction in village, farm is signposted.
Open: May until the August bank holiday weekend. Every day 12.00 pm - 5.00 pm. Admission charge. School tours by prior appointment.

The short summer months that the farm is open reflect the short but happy life-cycle of its inhabitants. In a humid hothouse at the rear of the farm you enter a mini-rainforest. Dodge the warm spray and try to find as many brilliantly coloured butterflies and moths as you can — and tot up how many stages of development you can spot. You can feed the adults on nectar and feel the silk on the cocoons of Giant Atlas Moths. In the main body of the building there are dead butterfly collections from all over the world, huge stick insect families, a python and some cuddly tarantulas and their dinners. (Local children provide). You can ask *any* questions about insects and arachnids, learn about cultivating your own caterpillars and buy some gifts at the little shop.

Morel Children's Farm, Straffan, Co. Kildare. Tel: 6288636.
Turn right for Straffan off Naas by-pass; take left at signposted
T-junction before the village. Admission charge. Open 10.00 am - 5.00
pm. every day.

It seems that all the rabbits that didn't make it to Australia came to
Morel Farm: the long-haired, lop-eared and exotic rabbits. Here too
you will find raccoons and marmosets, as well as the more common
goats, pigs, lambs, ducks, peafowl, Jersey calves, turkeys, guinea pigs
and several dozens of assorted fowl. The goat pens and rabbit pens
are open for visitors to wander through, and in the different seasons,
young animals can be bottle-fed. There's a stream picnic area, complete with sandy beach, as well as a snack bar off the farmyard.
Birthday parties are catered for (sausage and chips) by arrangement
and school tours also by prior arrangement. For others it's 10 - 5 pm
all year round, and there's a very leisurely atmosphere.

Bridestream Rare Breeds Farm, Kilcock, Co. Kildare. Tel: 6287261.
Leave Dublin/Galway road at AIB, Kilcock, through square, over
bridge, turn left at T-junction, and next right for the signposted
entrance.
Open from March to October, Wednesday to Sunday 2.00 pm - 6.00
pm. Other times and days by arrangement only. School tours by prior
arrangement.

The farm was established to rescue certain breeds of Irish and British
farm animals that were once common but are now nearly extinct. So
don't look for pink pigs and black and white Friesians here — you'll
find dainty Kerry cows, hairy red Tamworth pigs, 4-horned Manx
sheep, the 'extinct' Roscommon sheep and the prototype sheep called
the Soay. There's a horse museum with antique riding tackle and
horse-drawn machinery, a nature walk, play area and coffee shop.
Rabbit World is a warren for small visitors and, best of all, there are
pony rides galore. Birthday parties can be catered for, by arrangement.

Chapter 7

Inside Jobs

This is a short list of places that will let you in and show you how they work. It's short because some people wouldn't answer their telephone, others wouldn't say yes or no, and I didn't think of the rest. I didn't ask about free samples either — that's up to you.

Remember these points: (1) Most of these places will only take organised groups, and sometimes they specify how many, so you may have to work it through a school, a club, or a summer project. (2) People may be working when you get there, so don't do anything to get in their way. Keep any questions for the guide who is showing you around. (3) If you do get stuck in the machinery, remember I had nothing to do with it.

First of all I have listed public (or public funded) organisations that are part of the running of the country — and which are open to all, though sometimes needing a bit of postal homework beforehand. Individuals or families are welcome in these places. After that, the list is definitely one for groups, by arrangement, and details are briefer.

GOVERNMENT BUILDINGS AND THE TAOISEACH'S OFFICE, Merrion Street. What could be more hubbub and bustle than the seat of government, cabinet chambers and the Taoiseach's Office? Thanks to a new policy Government Buildings are open to the public on Saturdays from June 1992. The huge complex was once the science and engineering part of UCD, but in 1990 it was restored, using the finest Irish oak, beech and sycamore, by Irish craftspeople. Downstairs there's a gigantic state-of-the-art press theatre, and yes, you do climb the beautiful curved stairs to enter the Taoiseach's office. Breath in that powerful air! Admission is by ticket only and in groups of 16 only, with four tours every hour between 10.30 am and 4.45 pm (closed between 12.45 and 1.30). Tickets are available only from the National Gallery, down the road, and they are free.

THE BAILY LIGHTHOUSE is well worth a visit because it is the training lighthouse for lighthouse keepers, and it's the most accessible of the manned lighthouses. Gather a group together who are interested — not more than ten — with an adult as well. Write to the Commission for Irish Lights, Pembroke Street, Dublin 2, explaining your interest in visiting the Baily and when you would like to visit.

CIE do not show groups around the train engine works ... well, not unless you're a special case I didn't hear about. However, the public relations office at Connolly Station do send out special kits for train lovers — just write to the Media Officer, Connolly Station, Amiens Street, Dublin 1. (See also pages 133, 134)

You can visit the **LAW COURTS** around Dublin and see how Irish justice works. Everyone has seen court scenes in film and on television. The real thing is different in many ways. I do not recommend visits to all of the courts and, indeed, you may have to be with an adult to gain admission from the Clerk of the Court or the garda on door duty.

The big courts — the Supreme, the High and the Circuit — all sit in the Four Courts proper. They hear the criminal cases and the big civil cases and have juries. They sit during the law terms which are roughly the same as school terms and hearings start at 11.00 am and 2.30 pm (the morning sessions are the most lively). There is nothing going on during August and September or during Christmas and Easter holidays. The Legal Diary in the daily paper shows what cases are on in which courtroom on that day. It is doubtful that you would be allowed in. The District Court, round the east side of the Four Courts in Chancery Lane, may be more accessible. Here sits a lone judge handing down verdicts on driving offences and charges of unruly behaviour. This court sits all year round except for August and sessions start at 10.30 am. You can slip into the pews during sessions and leave without any bother. There are district courts at Bray, Dundrum, Dun Laoghaire, Howth, Kilmainham, Lucan, Rathfarnham and Swords which you can visit. Look up Part One of the telephone directory under Courts and telephone the office for the district court which you wish to visit, to make sure when it is sitting.

You can see how Irish democracy works by visiting **DÁIL ÉIREANN**. It sits on Tuesdays at 2.30 pm and Wednesdays, Thursdays and Fridays at 10.00 am. and most frequently during the months January to July so this is the time to plan your visit. Find out the names of the TDs for the constituency you live in (every constituency has at least three) by telephoning or writing to Dáil Eireann, Leinster House, Kildare Street (789911). Then telephone or write to the TD of your choice and explain that you wish to visit the Dáil. If you can arrange a group, family or otherwise, so much the better. Once you have the all-clear from the security check at the gate, you will be allowed into Leinster House and into the Visitors' Gallery. Your TD will probably take you there personally and will give you the printed proceedings for the day.

The more faces you can recognise, the more interesting it is looking into the debating chamber. Whether the speeches are stimulating or not, whether there is a full house or not, are matters of chance. Take time to look around and observe the strict format of Government and Opposition, ministers, spokesmen, front benchers, backbenchers and, above them all, the authoritative figure of the Cathaoirleach or Chairman. The press gallery is usually full, and you can check your own story against the Dáil reports in the papers and on the radio. The Senate chamber, a small, ornate hall at the other end of Leinster House, may also be visited. Leinster House is always a hive of bustle and business with sirens and bells sounding for Divisions and Quorums, and closed circuit television in the hall. The more you are interested in politics and personalities, the more exciting you will find it.

DUBLIN CORPORATION meetings are held in City Hall, Dame Street, on the first Monday of every month at 6.45 pm and you can get tickets to attend these meetings. Ring or write to Dublin Corporation, City Hall, Dame Street (6796111), and ask for the names and addresses of your local city councillors and then ring or write to one of them explaining why you want to attend. Each councillor has two tickets to give away for each meeting. Ask for the agenda of the meeting when you get there.

Mayor, aldermen (really means old men) and councillors will be there running the city for you like clockwork by telling the Corporation what to do with its bin lorries, shovels and library fine money. It could be a new road, a set of swings, or, in very lucky times, swag to go to a street theatre group that is up for discussion on the agenda. It's as good as the Muppet Show but you will really get a feeling of how the city is ticking over and growing all around you.

They argue a lot, these same councillors because (a) each has his/her own area to paint red before everybody else gets in on the act, and (b) because, just as in the Dáil, they all belong to different political parties. So it's pretty lively down in the Council chambers and, unlike the Dáil, you are only a few feet away from the gladiators. They don't wear fancy robes any more — ermine is definitely out — but the mayor does wear a chain and keeps order.

DUBLIN COUNTY COUNCIL, 46/49 Upper O'Connell Street (727777). The county council is responsible for all of County Dublin which is not looked after by Dublin Corporation, i.e. the non-citified parts. It meets on the second Monday of every month at 2.30 pm. You can get tickets to attend meetings in the same way as for Dublin Corporation, by ringing Dublin County Council and asking for the names of your councillors and then contacting them for a ticket. There are only ten seats in the public gallery.

DUNSINK OBSERVATORY, Castleknock (387911). Open September to March (i.e. autumn and winter when the nights are long), the first and third Saturday of each month, 8.00 pm to 10.00 pm. You need tickets which you can get by sending a stamped, addressed envelope to the Secretary at Dunsink Observatory, Castleknock, Co. Dublin. Admission free. Bus 40C from Parnell Street to Finglas South at the bottom of Dunsink Lane, half a mile from the observatory.

By night the observatory looks like a strange temple, by day very odd indeed, like the beloved folly of a mushroom grower. It is about 4 miles from the city as the crow flies, along the Royal Canal, and when it was founded in 1783, students and professors used to walk the distance — notably William Rowan Hamilton who suddenly penetrated a higher mathematical mystery while passing under one of the canal bridges (See page 27). Beaufort, who invented the scale for measuring wind speeds and gave new meaning to the life of weather forecasters, worked here for a while when he was 14 and his entries may be seen in the record books. (See page 132 for astronomy clubs.)

The **ESB** will show you what happens underneath the tall chimneys of a power station. Poolbeg Station arranges tours of the coal-fired station by appointment. You have to be over fourteen years of age. Apply to Poolbeg Power Station, Ringsend (685300). Turlough Hill near Glendalough is a hydro-electric scheme. Tours by arrangement. Telephone (0404) 45113.

IRISH FILM CENTRE, Eustace Street, Dublin 2. Tel: 778788 (subject to change). The Centre was not yet open when this edition was being prepared but by the time the book passes into your hands IFC may well be up and flourishing (from autumn 1992). What could be confirmed promised an exciting place for film enthusiasts, budding directors and film technicians and it will be an unrivalled education source with over 7,000 cans of Irish-made film in archives.

The building was for many years the city meeting-house of the Society of Friends, or Quakers. They actually assembled their building around a street courtyard called Coghill's Court, finally roofing over the street, and the new building has maintained this central courtyard atmosphere, adding a raised glass roof. There are two cinemas, a bar and restaurant, a shop and exhibition area. Special film exhibitions will be advertised in the newspapers. The Centre will be home to nine Irish film organisations, including the Junior Film Festival (See film entry in Joining In, page 126), the Irish Film Institute who house the archives, and Filmbase, a workshop and resource for young filmmakers. Primary and secondary teachers can check with the Institute's Education Officer how they can use the Centre. And if you've any interest in films check it out for yourself — it will be a great place to drop by!

For sheer fellow-feeling with the extra-terrestrials who will land here one day and have to try to figure us out, visit the **STOCK EXCHANGE**, 28 Anglesea Street, off Dame Street (778808). Admission is free but strictly by prior arrangement. School or club groups should write to Visitors' Enquiries and say what date, Monday to Friday, they would

care to visit. Entry is between 9.30 and 10.30 am. or between 2.15 and 3.00 pm. Interested individuals must make arrangements with a member of the Stock Exchange or with a stockbroker. The place is vastly entertaining for a short while and, if you get hooked, presumably you have what it takes to get on in the world of big business. At any rate it makes sense of the news ending, 'And here are the closing prices on the Dublin Stock Exchange...'

Downstairs is a huge blackboard with all the securities (companies) printed and various numbers chalked beside them. In an oval in the centre of the hall stockbrokers (all in suits and invariably male) shout out things, pick up telephones or rush around with notebooks. The President is at the top but the star of the show is the Registrar whose voice is a cross between Moses and Boris Karloff. He calls out securities and rings bells at unexplained moments. 'Moving Monopoly' is the best description of the whole carry-on.

Stockbroking proper began in Dublin in 1799 when an Act permitting 'proper persons only' to act as stockbrokers was drawn up. Its booms were in 1844-45 when railways began to creep across the country and believe it or not, in 1895 when there was a bicycle boom. Shareholders, who presumably had pedalled round past the Bank of Ireland, almost caused a riot in the Visitors' Gallery. The present building was built in 1878.

Even if you don't understand what's going on, it's worth a visit — it's good fun — and there's a nice little history that's free with your visit.

TEAGASC, 19 Sandymount Avenue, Dublin 4 (688188) is the national research, advisory and training organisation for the agriculture and food industry. They have 'Open Days' during the year at their two centres in the Dublin area: the National Food Centre at Dunsinea, Castleknock (383222) which investigates ideas in food production, and Kinsealy Research Centre, Malahide Road (460644) where horticultural developments are studied. Budding scientists, vets and gardeners would find visits fascinating. The Open Days are advertised in the national newspapers.

The **ABBEY THEATRE**, Lower Abbey Street, 1 (748741). Groups (by arrangement only) are shown around the Abbey Theatre during the day. You can see the inside, backstage, wardrobe and dressingrooms, as well as the Concorde-like lighting control room, and perhaps the odd famous face. Write or telephone the Abbey's Press Officer.

The **ARMY EQUITATION SCHOOL**, McKee Barracks, Blackhorse Avenue, 7 (774301). The school sometimes shows interested groups around the stables and showjumper training ground. Special arrangements must be made and the group would really have to be concerned with horses in some way. Your first query should be in writing.

The **CATTLE MARKET** (Ganly and Craigie's), Ashbourne Co. Meath. Tuesdays at 1 pm. You can just walk right into the Cattle Market, and see a special sort of auction at work. Not everybody's taste, but it is a good smelly spectacle. You have to resist the calves however. It's a bidding mart — the game is to see who is bidding and how. The auctioneers never hesitate so be careful not to scratch your nose, or you'll never know who'll be sharing the top bunk tonight. Wear wellingtons and jeans. The bus to Slane from Busarus will leave you at Ashbourne.

The **DUBLIN ART FOUNDRY**, 3A Rostrevor Terrace, 2 (760690). This foundry is where sculptors get their work cast. Huge and small sculptures in a tremendous noise of bronze. It's down near Grand Canal Basin. Groups, of less than ten, should ring for an appointment.

If you would like to see one of the oldest crafts still practised you should drop in at a **FORGE**. The smithy at Dunboyne, just beyond Blanchardstown, is over 200 years old. The fire is worked by a pump now, but the anvil, the nails, and certainly the horses are the same. Racehorses get light aluminium shoes, workhorses (very few of those guys) get clodhoppers.

FOSSETT'S CIRCUS, The Grange, Lucan, Co. Dublin (6280347). The circus has its winter headquarters in Lucan. They will sometimes do guided tours there, for groups by appointment only, between mid-November and mid-March. Their Dublin touring centres are: Booterstown, Dundrum and Whitehall, and tours can be arranged in any of these centres — again an appointment is necessary. A group tour could be combined with a visit to the circus.

IRISH STAINED GLASS LTD., Hanover Quay, 2 (773354). Will take up to fourteen accompanied *interested* secondary school pupils or art classes. By appointment only. There's crystal, church glass, and Georgian-style decorative glass.

THE IRISH TIMES, 31 Westmoreland Street, 2 (6792022). Shows groups around on Mondays and Tuesdays, by arrangement (maximum is six). Write or telephone the Production Manager. A newspaper office is an immensely exciting place, with people, stories and machines working at strange hours of the day. You will see the new computerised technology that most newspapers use nowadays. It prints vast amounts of newsprint in record time.

THE GEOLOGICAL SURVEY OF IRELAND, Beggar's Bush, Haddington Road, Dublin 4 (609511), is open weekdays, 2.30 pm - 4.30 pm, with school groups by arrangement. Down to Earth is the name of the GSI's exhibition open to the public. The Flintstones would find this the best-furnished place in Dublin with very handsome lumps of glistening granite and fiery basalt to lounge on and gold and septarian nodules to admire on the cave walls. Geology means knowledge of the earth's crust, and here it's the crumb of crust called Ireland that's on show. There are charts and maps going back to the good old days when things were boiling nicely and amoebae were threatening to do strange things. Ireland has some very ancient rocks and mountains — the Pre-Cambrian, as well as the very up-to-date peat bogs which, geologically speaking, are still in nappies and that's why they're damp too. You can speculate about the ancient continents of Laurasia and Gondwanaland and learn where Christmas tinsel comes from and become aware that your house is really made out of the earth, down to the paint and plaster. It also gives a feeling for the real beauty of stones. Fascinating for would-be scientists and artists.

SALESIAN AGRICULTURAL COLLEGE, Warrenstown, Drumree, Co. Meath (8259342). If you can imagine a farm school this is it. A lovely place that is both busy and quiet, and teaches everything from animal management to keeping accounts. They have an annual Open Day, usually in May, and advertised.

THE GENEALOGICAL OFFICE, 2 Kildare Street, Dublin 2 (618811). Here lieth the ways and means of discovering who your ancestors were, and, with luck, of fashioning a gigantic family tree. If you want to take this on as a family project you must be in earnest about the search (a) because genealogists are busy people and (b) because it will cost you money — though not necessarily a lot. An initial visit to the Heraldic Museum on the same premises will yield you some free pamphlets on the kind of details you'll need to start a genealogical search. After doing that groundwork you can get back to the Genealogical Office. (The hours are 10.00 - 12.45; 2.00 - 4.30 pm., Monday to Friday). There you can buy from them an Ancestry Tracing Research Pack (approx. £5). Or you can book a personal consultation with a researcher who will design a special tracing kit just suited to your family and the knowledge you have. This costs £10. Good luck!

ENFO — Information on the Environment, 17 St Andrew Street, Dublin 2. Tel: 6793144. Definitely a place for projects! ENFO is a pleasant walk-in resource centre (open Monday to Saturday, 10.00 am - 5.00 pm) crammed with leaflets on all aspects of the environment in this country. You can ask questions, use the library, watch videos, look at exhibitions and experiment with the computer software, which include re-designing the globe and the oceans. School groups are welcome but should book; individuals can just drop by.

SONAIRTE — National Ecology Centre, Laytown, Co. Meath. (041-27572) Open 9.30 - 5 in summer (may be extended after 1992). School groups by arrangement. The greenest of places, down by the serpentine river Nanny near the sea, Sonairte aims to show how conscience-clear energy alternatives work. Thus windmill power and a beautiful walled organic garden can be observed, and a walk taken on a nature trail by the river. The buildings and grounds rise phoenix-like from a tumbledown Big House and there's a lot of bricks and mortar work too. Courses take place here and it's a peaceful place for a picnic. Tea, coffee and snacks are available, and sometimes the garden produce.

NOTE: I would be delighted to hear from any other factories or organisations who will show visitors around their works. But readers should remember that if they have special interests like meteorology or map-making, say, and belong to a club or just make themselves known through correspondence, they stand a good chance of being admitted to the Ordnance Survey, or the Star-Wars-like Meteorological Office, places that do not normally admit visitors. They are just two examples. Use your head, and your neck to go places you want to go.

Chapter 8

BEACHES, ISLANDS, A BARBECUE AND BIRDS

People who live in capital cities like Dublin and Rio de Janeiro (Yes!) are lucky because there are sandy beaches a few miles out from the city centre. As a general rule Northside Dublin beaches are the better beaches, sandy and clean. They do get crowded though, and Southside beaches have other things to recommend them. So you or your family might be interested in breaking out of old Sunday traditions and trying some new beach to explore.

There are three (well two and a half) islands to be visited, one with its own king, birds to be noted and a recipe for a very easy beach barbecue — if you don't already have one.

Note: These excursions can be as lazy or as energetic as you wish: you can get a bus or train or you can walk or cycle all the way and spread yourself like a beached seal for the day. Over to you!

HOWTH

Buses: 31, 31A for Sutton, from Lower Abbey Street. DART.

You won't be the first person to discover Howth. Ptolemy, the fourth-century Roman geographer, put it on his map of the world as the island of Edros. (Sutton Cross is where Howth almost became an island). The Fianna were supposed to love the place and the Danes certainly did. The great thing about Howth is that it's always changing its face. In parts, it's as wild as Connemara, in others it's among the poshest places in Dublin, and it has the only castle in Dublin that's still lived in. But at the bottom of it all Howth is a fishing village.

Balscadden Beach — just past the harbour where the bus comes in. It's a small rather stony beach, but it's on the first leg of the climb to the summit, so if it's a warm day and you're going up, this is the only accessible beach for you.

Sutton Beach: It's on the other side of Howth facing south. It's sandy but very very shallow. There are lots of waders here, a spill-over from Bull Island. You can explore the rocks — good pools — and go right up to the Martello Tower. After this the Irish Sea currents open up so do not attempt to go further.

Howth Harbour: Is all new looking and finding its sea legs after some massive rebuilding. There is a fishing fleet and if you have the right manner or face, or whatever it takes, you might get taken on board a trawler for a look. It's a matter of asking questions — just takes nerve. In the mornings (weekdays) you can buy really fresh fish down here. And there's good fishing off the end of the pier for mackerel and pollock. Ireland's Eye is the island facing you and there *are* boat trips. (See Islands, page 119)

Howth Head

A proper cliff walk round Howth could take a whole day. You start the climb after Balscadden Bay. The road turns into a path and it's very easy to follow. On a clear day you can see the Mourne Mountains in County Down. But keep your eyes on the path and watch your dog if you have one. *Don't* go cliff climbing: it's extremely dangerous and there have been too many accidents already. Below you'll see Puck's Rock, a huge rock split in two. Legend has it that a devil fell here when

St Nessan waved a Bible at him. Further on is Casana rock, a proper caterwauling rock covered with seabirds. In May/July this part of the climb is covered with sea pinks and campions and is very beautiful. Don't pick them unless you live on a sea rock yourself. In 1855 the *Queen Victoria*, a steamboat, hit the rocks here in the middle of a snow-storm. On the inland side of the path are old quarries and lead mines.

As you reach the Summit you'll see the Baily Lighthouse down a slope guarding the entrance to Dublin Bay. It's the training house for lighthouse keepers. (See page 100). At the Summit there are all sorts of things you can do. You can give up and catch a bus down — into the village. Or you can walk down about 50 yards towards the Summit Inn and over the road you'll see some yellow bollards guarding the entrance to a grassy track. This is where the old Howth tram used to roll back down to the harbour. It was dismantled by wicked stepmother CIE in 1959. You can follow the track down.

Or if you want to go all the way to Sutton Strand, follow one of the paths towards the lighthouse and you'll find a path leading away to the right. There are more dramatic cliffdrops and in one place you can see how sand is made. Then catch the 31A bus back to town or explore the right-of-way paths around the Ben of Howth. This is the hill area to your left as you face the village. It is wild heathland, good practice for mountain walking. If you can get a map all the better, as the golf course seems to be expanding daily — you won't get lost but you might get hit by a ball.

Howth Castle

On the Dublin Road before you enter the village. The Castle is weird enough to have featured in one of the Dracula films. It's private and lived in by the descendants of the St Lawrences, but if your name is O'Malley you might try a knock. In 1575 the Lady Avenger, Granuaile (Grainne O'Malley), arrived on a social call but she was left at the gate because they were dining. Not being the sort to take this meekly she kidnapped the St Lawrence heir and took him on her ship back to Connacht, refusing to hand him over until she had the St Lawrence word that the gate would be open to all O'Malleys at mealtimes. You can wander around the grounds — if you're careful — because this is also the way to the golf club and rhododendron gardens. See if you can find the huge cromlech hidden in a bamboo grove — it's the grave of Aideen, a princess who got written about quite a lot. The Transport Museum is on your right. (See page 66)

PORTMARNOCK/MALAHIDE

Buses: 32/32A from Lower Abbey Street. Train from Connolly Station. Route: As for Howth, but turn before Sutton at Baldoyle Road and continue straight on.

Portmarnock is Dublin's nicest, nearest, beach — which you could tell anyway from its being called Velvet Strand. There are miles of strand, slight surf, breakwaters and donkey rides in summer. There is a small fair on the beach, and a crazy skyscraper Martello tower. On Sundays you can take off to the harness racing.

If you follow the beach round the curve to Malahide you leave some of the crowds behind — it gets rockier, and the beach isn't so perfect. But it's interesting to explore because (a) it's leading to the Malahide estuary which is always different and full of boat life and (b) you can hunt for fossils in the stretch of pale brown broken stones. And much nearer to Malahide itself (near the toilets) you'll find coral fossils, and brachiopods fixed in limestone rocks. They can be traced, if you're a fossil freak.

Malahide was a port town in medieval times. After the Dublin-Drogheda railway opened in 1844 it became a 'watering place' with promenades and military bands. Malahide Castle is worth a visit (page 69) and also St Doulagh's miniature abbey (page 67).

DONABATE/PORTRANE

Bus: 33B from Eden Quay. Train from Connolly Station. Route: Swords Road and signposted turn.

Donabate is a wonderful beach with miles of dunes. It *is* that bit far away — a trip needs an early start. Portrane is just beyond Donabate, on the same bus route. You go through Donabate, keeping left. You can stay with the sandy beach at the head of the village or, for the caves, take the right turn by the sea and go to the end, to the Martello tower. These little shingle beaches are *not* for bathing; they're not particularly attractive either, but *when the tide is fully out and only then*, you can go down and explore the caves. Because the sea fills them at high tide, you'll find sea anemones clinging like wine gums to the cave walls and roofs. You'll also find white shreds, hanging spookily and batlike from the roof. Examine this find carefully — it's what Nature has made out of human nature. The cliff path walk to

Donabate carries a safety warning. Just in front of this beach a tragic sea-wrecking happened in 1854 — you'll find the details in the Civic Museum (page 52). Don't go here without adult supervision and *always* remember the tides. The island is Lambay, which is not within reach of ordinary mortals. (See Islands, page 120).

Because of the dunes these beaches are ideal for barbecues on summer evenings. Here is a very simple barbecue menu that works well for everywhere.

Bring (for ten people) 3 lbs of sausages; 10 bread rolls buttered; 10 tomatoes; tomato ketchup; 2 large onions (optional); 1 packet of margarine for frying; apples; chocolate biscuits; minerals; frying pan (large); and at least *one* knife.

Everything should fit into four rucksacks which can be shared around. For fire, either cheat and bring a camping stove, or bring matches, firelighters and newspapers. Choose a sheltered dune area. Find flat stones from someone else's barbecue and make a square hearth that your frying pan will sit on. Collect twigs, paper rubbish and any driftwood from along the beach and build a fire. When the fire is well lit and glowing, melt the margarine in the pan and fry the sausages and tomatoes. Stick them in the buttered rolls with sauce and some raw onion. It's very fast and the food will be gorgeous. You can keep the fire going for warmth if you've collected enough fuel, but make sure the sparks are completely extinguished before you go and clear away any mess that isn't burnt.

LOUGHSHINNEY

Bus: 33 from Eden Quay very rarely goes via Loughshinney so this should be a car or bike trip. Route: Swords — turn for Lusk and follow Loughshinney signpost. Or is it Lough Shinney? I've seen both!

Loughshinney is more difficult to find than Rush or Skerries, which you can also visit on the 33 bus route, but it's a scaled down and interesting place that you could get very attached to. And not *too* many people know about it.

There is a perfect miniature harbour and a safe life-guarded beach that very small children adore. And because it's all quite small the water heats quickly, like a rock pool. The houses come right down to the beach and their gardens rise in a higgledy-piggledy sort of way. There are great rock pools beyond the harbour and the cliffs look like moon cliffs. There was a geological crusher phase in the distant past which helped to produce these Ryvita-like rock formations. On the walk to the left you pass by earthworks of an ancient promontory fort — you can try to be an aerial photographer on the ground.

The **Southside Beaches** start very near the city, at Sandymount, and go all the way down to the bottom of Ireland. But this book stops at Bray, or almost. The DART from Pearse Station will take you to all the beaches. There are also buses to each of them. The bicycle ride to Dun Laoghaire from town will take nearly an hour depending on the wind, so if you want to go there or further on your bicycle I suggest you start early in the morning.

SANDYMOUNT STRAND

Buses: 2 or 3 from Townsend Street. DART.
It's a huge strand, great for walks with dogs, for castle building and beachcombing, but not for swimming. When the tide is out, you have to walk miles to the shoreline; when it's in you can see all manner of unpleasantness floating around. On the beach you can go in to see the old sea baths, looking a bit decayed now, like an old Moorish fort. From the tower up to Merrion used to be a high class bathing area in the last century, with rows of brightly painted bathing boxes. All along the stretch of strand from Sandymount to Blackrock you can see the over-flow of waders from Bull Island, and other people shell-fishing or worm-digging. If you like cockles and lug-worms, away you go. My advice is not to eat the cockles, however, just to save the shells.

BOOTERSTOWN

Buses: 7A, 8, 45. DART. There is a tiny bird sanctuary between the road and the railway. It's a miniature slob with a causeway for viewing. A noticeboard with portraits of the inhabitants will tell you what to look out for, but the resident heron can often be seen from the bus. Booterstown Common usually houses either a large fun-fair during the summer months, or one of Ireland's three circuses. Camels have been seen grazing wild on the football pitch.

This coast road to Blackrock, believe it or not, used to be a favourite carriage drive for wealthy Dublin families in the eighteenth century, and, naturally enough, it came to be patronised by highwaymen, the real kind, with masks and pistols. Letters to the papers about road conditions were even juicier in those days — and they even had groups of vigilantes set up to patrol the road from Baggot Street to Blackrock.

BLACKROCK

Buses: 7A, 8, 45. DART. In the middle ages there used to be a road from Poolbeg to Blackrock across the sands. The mayor and Corporation of medieval Dublin established the boundary of the city along this road. They would throw out a javelin as far as they could to mark the outer limits of their franchise. The Blackrock franchise or boundary stone can still be seen in the main street outside the Central Café.

Take the beach from Blackrock towards Seapoint. You will find it difficult to go all the way because a rather mean individual has closed off access where the old Seapoint Baths used to be. However, there is a jewel of a little beach with beautiful shells along here and you will pass some strange little temple-like structures and a tiny look-alike of Nero's baths. They were built in 1834 by the railway company for the Earl of Cloncurry as compensation for building the railway to Dun Laoghaire through the Earl's property and it marked the end of Blackrock as a fashionable resort of the eighteenth century!

SEAPOINT

Buses: 7A, 8, 45. DART. Go through Blackrock, take the Coast Road, then about a quarter of a mile down Seapoint Avenue you will find an excellent swimming area. The water is deep around the rocks at high tide, but there's an ordinary slope from the strand. Canoeing and windsurfing are other options here (see Joining In, pages 138, 140). The rocky stretch on the left has plenty of cormorants, turnstones and gull types who moved in when the baths closed. Seapoint Martello Tower would have drawn Napoleon to Ireland if he had any means of knowing how good the ice-cream in the tower shop tastes after a swim. Napoleon may not have come to grief here but, incredible as it seems, all along the stretch where people paddle, there is a long history of horrible shipwrecks. The building of the railway got rid of the worst of the rocks.

Cormorants

DUN LAOGHAIRE HARBOUR

Buses: 7A, 8, 46A. DART. If you go to Dun Laoghaire on the train you're following the first railway ever built in Ireland. It was built in 1834. Then it was called the Dublin-Kingstown railway and it was made to stop at the west pier and come no further because people were afraid it might run amok in the town.

The best way to see the harbour is to go straight out on to one of the piers. The first one is the west pier. The piers are quite different both in appearance and in clientele and you can develop a pet pier. The west pier is on the Dublin side of the harbour. It's wilder and quieter, with long grass, and much frequented by fishermen and dogs. It's a fair walk out one pier and back but at the end you can see Dublin Bay curved round like a bill hook. The lighthouses at the ends of the piers are unmanned and, of the lightships you can see moored, one is a replacement ship (the *Codling*) and the other is used by sea scouts for training. Near the west pier is the Coal Quay; it is part of the original Dun Laoghaire, having been built in 1767. Fishing trawlers put up here, and there's always maintenance work going on — hence the several ships' chandlers in the main street.

The east pier is past the yacht clubs, the Mail Boat jetty and lifeboats. It's the Family Pier. In summer there are boat trips around the bay leaving from this pier. The seaward side of the pier is a rocky embankment which can be climbed on or fished from (for codling, bass and eel). There are sea baths here facing the People's Park. They were built for Victorian bathers and boasted all the niceties sure to satisfy even 'the most fastidious invalid'; seaweed baths, and separate tanks for ladies and gentlemen were listed among the perks.

But take heart at the very un-Victorian looking snake tubes at the back of the swimming baths. These are the Rainbow Rapids — giant slippery chutes that deposit persons into deliciously warm water. Payment is per number of descents, the more the cheaper per ride. Open in summer. It's privately owned: the baths are Corporation owned. The whole area may be developed for water sports.

It's worth leaving the seafront and going up town to see the shops. The shopping centre is a proper palace, set out in galleries after the style of the old Lancashire/Yorkshire arcades. On and off George's Street there are all sorts of food shops, a craft shop, second-hand clothes shops and a second-hand bookshop. Dun Laoghaire also has the Maritime Museum. (See Museum chapter, page 62)

Sandycove beach is easily seen from Dun Laoghaire and it's considered to be a beach suitable for women and children, while the deep swimming place round the corner under the tower is for 'Forty-foot gentlemen only'. That's what it says. The beach is *very* dirty but small children seem to love it. You can go into this Martello tower because it is the James Joyce museum. (See page 62)

DALKEY

Bus: 8. DART. Route: Dun Laoghaire, Sandycove, Dalkey.
Dalkey is about $2^1/_2$ miles from Dun Laoghaire. It's not a beachy place, more one for messing about in boats or watching them. This tradition goes back to the days when it was Dublin's trading port — from about 1200 AD to 1600. There are two small harbours, Bullock and Coliemore.

The first harbour, Bullock harbour, is before the town. It has a fine busy-boat atmosphere in summer and there is a huge marine emporium on the old stone quay. Rowing boats and outboard engined boats can be hired in good summer weather. Rock from Dalkey quarry used to be shipped out from here, and there are huge rocks behind the sea wall to be explored. If you catch a fish you don't have to give one to the castle behind — which used to be the fee the Cistercian monks who lived there charged for fishing the waters.

Coliemore harbour (through the village and down Coliemore Road) is the old port of Dalkey — though it was a pretty rough place, the cargo was unloaded onto rocks which were called Salt Rock, Corn Rock and Coal Rock. The obvious place to head for is the island. (See page 118)

Dalkey village is a pretty place and because it was Dublin's port it had the amazing number of seven castles — Goat's Castle is the town hall.

Note: You can walk to or from Dun Laoghaire to Dalkey by a special path called 'The Metals'. When the rock from Dun Laoghaire harbour was being quarried in Dalkey, between 1817 and 1867, the rock used to be whizzed down in trucks on metal tracks. The full ones going down pulled the empty ones going back — a proper funicular railway. 'The Metals' starts beside the railway on the waterfront in Dun Laoghaire.

KILLINEY

Bus: 59 from Dun Laoghaire station. DART. Route: Dalkey, Coliemore Road, Vico Road.

Killiney has several beach places. The train leaves you at the main beach while the walk up the Vico Road is wonderful with rocks and sea and distant small boats and strawberry pink houses overhanging the cliffs. There is an entrance to the right which will bring you to the hill park. (See Parks, page 92). Steps on the left will take you to the White Rock bathing place — for good swimmers. There is a small beach past the railway bridge which is the place to come in winter to watch storms and spray. To the left of the footbridge is Decco's cave, called after an Italian who used to live in the cave. It was originally the opening to a lead mine in Killiney Hill.

The main beach is very long, a bit stony, but good for swimming and shore fishing. There are nice grassy dunes and mounds. You could travel alongside the railway track all the way to Bray.

BRAY

Bus: 45 from Poolbeg Street. DART. Route: to Donnybrook, Stillorgan, Foxrock, Shankill, Bray.

Bray has a pretty awful beach, but then it's got Bray Head which was made to be climbed, several amusement palaces and the National Aquarium. (See page 63)

The promenade is a very old-fashioned affair. It goes well with all the hotels and guest-houses facing. In Victorian Dublin, Bray was the place to come on your half-day off per month if you were 'in service'. That's how the amusements grew up — and there are still dodgems, ghost trains, palm-reading, fish and chips, candy floss and one-armed bandits.

Bray Head is not a difficult climb but the vegetation changes, from blackberries and ferns to a pine glade, to rock, make it seem like a little Alp. You can see Wales on a clear day, and some of the Wicklow mountains. The walk to Greystones is four miles — if you are tempted.

Or you can follow the track by the railway. The building of the track through solid rock is a smallish marvel though it put an end to Bray smugglers who had an Ali Baba cavern underneath, known as the Brandy Hole.

ISLANDS

All coasts have islands and so has Dublin. Exploring an island, picnicking in what might well be a smuggler's cove, looking for all the different kinds of flora and fauna that flourish away from the car pollution and the citizenry, is a real thrill that can be yours any good spring or summer's day. (In winter too, see number $3^1/_2$ below). There are three and a half islands on this agenda. The first two are perfect specimens. Bring warm clothes, no matter how hot it is, and food.

DALKEY ISLAND

Ferries go to the island from Coliemore Harbour. No regular service or boatman — ask a fisherman. Price by arrangement.

There are rowing boats for hire at the harbour, but you would need to have an excellent adult oarsperson — though the island looks very close this is deceptive, because you have to travel diagonally against the cross currents. So stick to the ferry is the best advice.

Once you land on the rocky shore you are under the jurisdiction of 'His Facetious Majesty, King of Dalkey, Emperor of the Muglins, Prince of the Holy Island of Magee, Elector of Lambay and Ireland's Eye, Defender of His Own Faith and Respector of all Others, and Sovereign of the Lobster and the Periwinkle.' The King of Dalkey is quite benign however, and there's no customs so you're free to range all over. There are lots of rabbits and, until recently, beautiful wild goats that looked just like Icelandic sweaters, grey and brown and shaggy. There is a ruined seventh-century church that belonged to St Begnat once but is now the goats' shelter. At one end of the island is an old magazine fort, which like the nearby martello tower was built to keep a weather eye out for Napoleon. The story goes that the soldiers were forgotten about after Napoleon was defeated at Waterloo, and they stayed on Dalkey Island for forty years waiting for a French invasion. The rocks out to sea are the Muglins and in 1766 two pirates were executed and their bodies chained to the Muglins as an example.

IRELAND'S EYE

Ireland's Eye is reached by ferry from Howth Harbour. Boats leave in summer hourly, or on demand, from a signposted stage on the further pier. Last return boat leaves the island about 6.00 pm. It's not cheap, so plan on making a full day trip. Bring all food and drink — there's no shop on the island.

It's bigger than Dalkey Island, but it's a democracy and has not got goats. It has cliffs with lots of seabirds, like Howth, so the same cautions apply. Gannets have recently begun to breed here. *Don't go cliff climbing or egg collecting.* There was a time when goshawks used to breed here — they were a falconer's bread and butter sort of hawk. Centuries ago too, the old reliable ruined church (St Nessan's) and Martello tower were built. St Nessan's was always being broken up by pirates, so in the end it was abandoned. Pirates may or may not have used the caves on the eastern end of the island, seals don't, they apparently prefer Lambay. The centre of the island is carpeted in bracken, jungly but surmountable (and an excellent toilet facility). On the side facing Howth there's a beach that's pleasant to swim from and watch the weekend sailing. Some boatpeople come no farther than the Eye, moor and drink beer or champagne — lazy lot!

LAMBAY ISLAND

Lambay Island is really here under false pretences. It's privately owned, but *very, very* occasionally permission has been granted for interested groups (like a naturalists' club) to visit. It's situated north of Ireland's Eye, just out from Rush, and has an extraordinarily rich wild life. Anyway, just on the off-chance, the address to write to is: Lord Revelstoke, Lambay Island, Rush, County Dublin.

BULL ISLAND AND DOLLYMOUNT BEACH

Bus: 30 from Lower Abbey Street.

Bull Island is the half-island on the list. It really is an island, but there is a wooden causeway at one end, and a bona fide road at the other, crossing the water and sludge — so most visitors do not feel like intrepid explorers. Yet Bull Island has got more wildlife in its little toe, so to speak, than many an Atlantic run-wild, run-free beach. It also has the most popular beach in Dublin, Dollymount beach, and a golf course, the Royal Dublin.

It's a completely artificial island. Get off at the wooden causeway, walk over, and you see the Bull Wall stretching ahead with a lighthouse at the end. The wall was built in 1825 (with some help from Captain Bligh of the mutinous *Bounty*. See also the Maritime Museum, page 62) to make a deep channel going up into Dublin port. A sandbank built up behind the wall, and the bigger it got the more things grew there — until finally there was the Amazing Tale of the Bull Island Mouse.

The Bull Island Mouse was discovered and found to be pale and sandy, unlike field mice or sober dark Dublin house mice. So just about when Charles Darwin published his *Origin of Species,* the Bull Island mouse was trotted on as a witness for Darwin — to prove that animals did adapt and evolve to survive. It was all very exciting.

The beach is just to the left of the wall and stretches for 3 miles. It's not peaceful, but it's a very good sandy beach, with dunes all along. The seawater is cleaner than at Sandymount, which is also near to the city centre, but don't expect great things of the water.

The marvellous thing about the Bull is the horde of birds that don't care in the least that they're surrounded by city rather than water. So, if you want to go nature-spotting, face in to land, rather than out to sea. Take wellingtons, an anorak, a pocket bird book and a pair of binoculars, if you can get them. If you come in on the bona fide road

(nearer to Howth) you can acclimatise yourself by dropping in at the Interpretative Centre at the roundabout. It's open from 10.00 am to 4.30 pm. The video will show you what to look out for; the display boards will give you the Identi-kit details from lowly worm to highly lark. You'll get an idea why the Island was created a UNESCO biosphere. But if you come in on the causeway, or you want practice before theory, turn left at the Sea Scouts shed on the Bull Wall, just after the cottages. Among the birds you will see walking about on the saltmarsh are curlews, dunlins, herons, knots, plovers, red and green-shanks, sanderlings, turnstones. These waders are just crazy about their mudpie diet, but in order that they won't fight over the same worm, notice how they all have varied leg lengths for wading at different depths and different length bills for digging in different layers.

Out on the water you will see geese from Greenland (in winter), swans and an assortment of ducks. On land larks and pippits are very common, and you might see a short-eared owl, kestrels (spot the kestrel and bat nesting boxes on the telephone poles), sparrowhawks, merlins, or the fabled peregrine falcon, who *has* been spotted, no doubt watching the golf like a hawk. (He might well do, there are plans to eat into wild area to make more room for golfers.)

On land you might also be lucky enough to see a hare (some of whom cross over the mud at low tide in autumn). They are shy and should not be introduced to your dog. You might also see a wolf-spider, a cuckoo-spit bug, a snail-killing fly, a spider-hunting wasp, a dune-robber fly or a hairy wood-louse. And if you don't think you could see any of these creatures, but would like to, why not go on a field trip with a club? (See page 146)

Note: We didn't include a chapter on Dublin 'mountains' because the book would have been impossibly long if we had tackled the huge range of walks and climbs within striking distance. And it has been done very well by somebody else. Let someone in the family buy a copy of *On Foot: Exploring the Wilderness in Dublin and Wicklow* by Christopher Moriarty, or *Hill Strolls around Dublin* by David Herman, available from all good bookshops. The second book has 24 climbs, all with maps, times and distances. He mentions which climbs are not suitable for dog company (sheep), which need waterproof clothing, which are easy, which are Himalayan. But the Golden Rule is: always travel in company and tell someone where you intend to go.

Chapter 9

JOINING IN

This chapter means just that. All of the societies and associations listed are glad to hear from young people: some of them are entirely youth-centred. Many welcome families, others (and this is great if you are a bit shy) give you facilities and information to get on with your own particular bug on your own terms. Whether you want to build a telescope or get a mate for your Shitzu, are sporty, or superstitious, this chapter has tried to fit you in somewhere. It's a reference chapter, so at the end you will find lists — swimming pools, tennis courts, libraries. But before you get that far, with any luck you will have started wondering why you thought all the good things happened to someone else, somewhere else...

Note: Where just a private address and number are given, this is a contact, usually an annually elected secretary, who will give you the information you need. So, if you write for information *do* enclose a stamped addressed envelope.

CREATION! From Art to Science

ART
Dublin Corporation run art and craft classes in various city and suburban centres, mainly libraries. Contact Youth Information Centre, Sackville Place for details (786844) or the Central Library, Cumberland House, Fenian Street, 2 (619000)/The National Gallery sometimes run painting holidays and workshops — ask the Education department (615133)/Pine Forest Art Centre in Rathfarnham have both summer and year-round classes for different age-groups in various aspects of art and crafts, with portfolio work for older

students. A bus picks up students from various southside pick-up points (2955598) / City Arts Centre, 23/25 Moss Street, 2, at the Matt Talbot Bridge is a focal point for visual arts, in the display of new work (including computer art) and in community involvement. Schools and groups are welcome to work with the Education Officer. (770643) — they also have an excellent restaurant/Wet Paint Arts, Basement, 17 Herbert Street, 2, have programmes in arts education, community projects and they have an arts information service — see Drama also (611757).

DANCE

Classical Ballet requires classical training. For a complete list of all teachers and schools conforming to the Royal Academy of Dance, contact Mrs. Jill O'Neill, Irish Administrator, 9 Ruby Hall, Rochestown Avenue, Dun Laoghaire (2808874). There are teachers throughout Dublin, and boys and girls from 6 years upwards are welcome / The Irish National College of Dance, Blackrock (2859294) has a ballet school which is affiliated to a ballet company, the Dublin City Ballet, so students get a good idea of the life of a professional dancer. Various age levels from 6 up.

Ballet classes are also held in the following dance centres: Dance Centre, Digges Lane, 2 (784288); Dublin School of Classical and Contemporary Dance, 13 Stamer Street, Portobello, 8 (543355).

Contemporary/Jazz
Dublin School of Classical and Contemporary Dance, 13 Stamer Street, Portobello, 8 (543355); The Granby Dance Works, 10 Granby Place, 1 (721812); Dance Theatre of Ireland, Digges Lane, 2 (784205).

Disco
Beginners Dance Centre, NBU Hall, 54 Parnell Square, 1 (304647) — junior disco.

Irish Dancing
The administration is by Coimisiún Rince, 6 Harcourt Street, 2 (752220) who will give local teachers and schools.

Variety Dancing/Singing
The Billie Barry Dancing School specialises in getting children on stage in variety shows and pantomimes. Contact 16 St Declan's Rd, 3 (339644).

DRAMA & THEATRE

For reference only, not for artistic purposes, I have divided this section so that Drama means acting, directing, mime, backstage work — all those things, and Theatre means audience entertainment.

Drama

Three city centre schools are: Gaiety School of Acting, 25 Suffolk Street, 2 (6799277); Betty Ann Norton Theatre, Studio 27, Harcourt Street, 2 (751913); The Performing Arts School, Digges Lane, 2 (784288) all of which offer different options for different age-groups. Summer courses are held in the first two. Irish Children's Theatre Group, 19 Whitebarn Road, Churchtown, 14 (2986636): classes in all aspects of drama for the young. The 'group' is a separate component and involves large numbers of children in workshops and productions and exchanges abroad.

School-leavers can apply for VEC courses in Theatre Studies in Coolock, Inchicore and Marino. Enquiries to: 680614.

Dublin Youth Theatre, 23 Upper Gardiner Street, 1 (743687) holds auditions every year for its company of 14-22-year-olds. Workshops are held on Saturdays and at least four public productions are staged every year.

The National Association for Youth Drama (NAYD) also at 23 Upper Gardiner Street, (743687) is a co-ordinating body for youth theatre in Ireland. They organise courses, run the National Youth Theatre and the National Youth Drama Festival and work with European Youth Encounter. They will supply on request a list of local youth theatre groups in Dublin city and county.

Wet Paint Arts, Basement, 17 Herbert Street, 2 (611757) work closely with young people's theatre in different areas of Dublin — ask for particulars.

Note: There are many other local youth drama groups, both community based and those attached to adult amateur drama groups. Dublin Libraries have published a very useful list of arts organisations and it can be consulted in any library.

Theatre

TEAM education theatre, 4 Marlborough Place, 1 (786108). TEAM go to you, not you to them — i.e. it is a school touring company, based in Dublin and visiting nine other counties with original plays. They have workshops too and involve the audience in playing with a chosen theme.

Iomha Ioldánach, 5/6 Capel Street, 1 (722106) visit primary schools with their original plays based on themes and stories from Irish mythology. Their work is bilingual (either/or, or both) and they also perform in street theatre productions.

Down to Earth Theatre Company, Hogan House, Hogan Place, Grand Canal Street, Dublin 2 (613022) produce original plays with environmental themes for primary schools and community youth groups. They also offer workshops.

The Lambert Puppet Theatre, Clifton Lane, Monkstown (2800974) is run by master puppeteer Eugene Lambert and his large family. The shows are varied, touring in winter, but with matinée shows in Dublin every Saturday. The theatre has a collection of over 300 puppets and marionettes.

CAFE — Creative Arts for Everyone — 23/25 Moss Street, 1 (770330) is a resource group with a register of entertainers in the dramatic arts who are available for school or community performances.

Occasionally plays with juvenile interest are performed seasonally in almost all Dublin theatres. The Dublin Theatre Festival in October usually introduces at least one internationally acclaimed youth production, as well as mime and street theatre.

FILM / MEDIA

The Irish Film Institute runs the annual Junior Film Festival in autumn at the Film Centre in Eustace Street, 2.

A media summer school for school-leavers is held in Ballyfermot Senior College during June, July and August. Enquiries to: 6269421.

UCI cinema complexes in Tallaght, Coolock, and Santry Omniplex, hold a Saturday morning special film show (adults free!). Information in newspapers or from the cinemas.

MUSIC

Dublin has always been super-rich in music training and this section could be pages longer. I have to choose a range of options but the list could be (and I hope will be) added to indefinitely.

Centre-city Music Schools: These schools teach all levels in all the classical orchestral instruments, in singing, music theory and appreciation. Groups are often formed within the schools. College of Music, Chatham Row (778820) has an extension in the VEC, Ballyfermot (265901) / Royal Irish Academy of Music, 36 Westland Row (764412) / Leinster School of Music, 5 Upper Stephen Street (751532) / Walton's College of Music, 2 North Frederick Street (786938).

Local Music Teachers do not have an association, but since many are attached to one of the first three colleges on the list above, a query for a *local* piano, strings or brass teacher will usually be answered. The Golden Pages lists only a small number under Music Teachers. Your local library or community centre may also be able to help.

Music for Very Young Children: The Suzuki violin method which teaches ages 2-5 how to love and handle a violin has a few teachers in Dublin. For names, contact Mrs Goor, Annacrivey House, Enniskerry, Co. Wicklow (2868297) / Newpark Music Centre, Newtown Park Avenue, Blackrock, Co. Dublin (2883740) teaches: violin, 'Discovering Music' for 4-7 years and recorder groups (6+).

Irish Traditional Music
Comhaltas Ceoltoirí Éireann, 32 Belgrave Square, Monkstown, Co. Dublin (2800295). They teach tin whistle to children on Saturday mornings and their classes in fiddle, flute, accordion are for all from age 7 upwards. Also check out music schools.

Wind and Brass
The Irish Youth Wind Ensemble (minimum standard grade 6) give concerts and have a summer school for players. Write to: Mrs. Eileen Kavanagh, 37 Slievebloom Park, Dublin 12. A contact for brass and concert bands is the Irish Association of Brass and Military Bands, $^c/_o$ Joe Shiels, 6 Mount St. Oliver, Drogheda, Co. Louth, or, for marching bands, Tallaght Youth Band, $^c/_o$ St Mary's School, Greenhills Road, Dublin 24. Instrumental training is given in all youth bands.

Jazz/Rock
Newpark Music Centre, Blackrock (2893740) teach sax, guitar, drums, the language of jazz performance/Ballyfermot Senior College (6269421) teach rock music and rock management as a third-level course.

Orchestra

The National Youth Orchestra of Ireland has 300 members in two sections — Junior (11-16) and Senior (16-21). Both give concerts and go on tour. There are twice-yearly residential rehearsal sessions. Auditions of new members are held in the autumn, in strings, woodwind, brass and percussion. Send details about yourself and your music training to: National Youth Orchestra of Ireland, 37 Molesworth Street, 2 (613642).

The Dublin Orchestras for Young Players play all year round, give concerts, run a summer school and organise European exchanges. Contact Mrs Crooks, 62 Ailesbury Grove, Dublin 16 (2980680) / West Dublin Youth Orchestra has two age-groups playing. Contact Mrs Hudson (8212141) / Young European Strings is a training in orchestral experience for players in three age-groups from 4 to 12. There are rigorous weekly sessions and occasional performances. Contact Maria Kelemen, 21 The Close, Cypress Downs, Templeogue, 6W (905263).

Choral Music

There are choristers (boys only) in St Patrick's Cathedral (for pupils of the Cathedral school only), St Ann's, Dawson Street, St Bartholomew's, Clyde Road, and the Pro-Cathedral (the Palestrina Choir). You need an exceptional voice. Other churches have less formal choir arrangements — ask locally.

Newpark Music Centre, Blackrock (2893740) have two choral classes, 'Let's All Sing' for 6-9-year-olds and Cantino for 10-14-year-olds.

There are many local young people's choirs. A few well-known ones to try are: Cór na nÓg, who perform with the National Symphony Orchestra (write to the director, Colin Mawby, at RTE Studios, Portobello, 8, for an audition) / Dublin Boy Singers, open to boys over 7 by audition. Contact Frank Hughes, 203 Grange Road, Rathfarnham, 16 (2945506) / The Young Lindsay Singers and Linettes (girls only, under 18s and under 12s). Information from Ethna Barror (304320) / Parc Singers has a youth group for girls only and a mixed junior group. They meet in the city centre. Contact Sean Creamer, 34 Abbey View, Monkstown, Co Dublin (2802064).

An overall address for queries about local choirs is: Association of Irish Choirs, Drinan Street, Cork.

Other useful addresses: Feis Ceoil, 37 Molesworth Street, 2 (613642) / Music Association of Ireland, 5 North Frederick Street, 1 (746060) / Slógadh, 26 Merrion Square 2 (767283).

The *Irish Times* operate, in conjunction with the RTE orchestras, a Music in the Classroom programme. Contact Sean Hogan at the *Irish Times* very early in the school year — it gets booked up almost immediately. Ceol Cumann na n-Óg organise a 'young person's guide to the orchestra' lecture for schools (2841694).

Musician of the Future/Singer of the Future
In alternate years, talented young classical musicians and singers compete in these prestigious competitions. Details from RTE Music Department, RTE, 4.

SCIENCE

The RDS, Ballsbridge, 4 (680645) have a Youth Science Officer, provide the venue for the Aer Lingus Young Scientists Exhibition, run a Youth Science and Arts week every summer and a club for boffins called the Electron Club (a Dun Laoghaire man introduced the concept of the electron and its name, in 1891). Meetings are held and there is a regular newsletter. Enquiries to the Youth Science Officer, as above.

DUBLIN PUBLIC LIBRARIES

Dublin libraries are busy places, with activities for children ranging from exhibitions to drama, from story-telling to fancy dress. Not all of the activities listed are available in all libraries: space and staff vary from library to library. If you are interested in any particular activity check with your local library for details. (See list and phone numbers at the end of this chapter.)

Arts and Crafts: which means anything from drawing and collage to painting big beautiful wall murals or making junk sculpture. Some libraries give scrolls, others exhibit your work / *Book Clubs:* in most libraries, with discussions and quizzes / *Drama Workshops:* in libraries with room / *Exhibitions:* include the display of children's art and writing and books of special interest / *Music Listening Facilities:* Audio and music cassette tapes to plug into on the premises / *Project Files:* A lot of libraries have built up a collection of Project Files to help with hobbies and schoolwork. Ask at the desk / *Quizzes:* The Dublin Inter-library Quiz takes place each summer. Quiz heats take place in local libraries during the year / *Slide Shows and Film Strips:* Available to teachers and youth club leaders / *Story-telling:* in most libraries, for younger children. On fine days can be outside / *Children's Book Week:* towards the end of October is actually two weeks of mad activity in libraries, with competitions, author interviews, fancy dress and more.

SUMMER PROJECTS AND SUMMER CAMPS

Summer Projects are free holiday activities/workshops/excursions — based in schools usually, but that's for convenience not for similarity. If you don't know about your local Summer Project through your school, contact the Dublin Corporation Youth Information Centre, Sackville Place (786844) or the Catholic Youth Council, 20-23 Arran Quay (725055), either of which will tell you all you need to know.

Summer Camps (the Dublin-based ones) vary greatly. Some are quite academic and are pointedly intended for catching up on school work: others are more like Summer Projects, some are conducted through Irish, others again are quite like their American counterparts. All are fee-paying. Some regulars include: Eurosport, based at UCD Belfield sports complex (soccer, fencing, tennis, archery, basketball): 2809451; Camp Blackrock, based in Blackrock College (most sports including swimming, drama, arts and computer workshops): 2888681; Camp Portmarnock, based at Portmarnock Sports and Leisure Club, (most sports, swimming and soccer camps): 8462122; Newpark Venture Camp, based at Newpark Comprehensive School, Blackrock (most sports, with specialised swimming): 2883720; Camp Glenalbyn, based at Glenalbyn House, Stillorgan (sports, swimming, and knock-out activities): 2880857. Special interest summer courses for young people include **Drama** - Gaiety School of Acting, Suffolk Street (6799277); Betty Ann Norton Summer Drama, St Louis School, Rathmines (751913); Andrews Lane Acting School, Andrews Lane (6797760); **Art** - Pine Forest Summer School, Rathfornham (2955598). There are many more courses available each year — consult your local newspapers and sports complexes. Papers will also carry details of out-of-Dublin residential adventure camps and Gaeltacht holidays.

THE BIG YOUTH ORGANISATIONS

These organisations do not fall into any special category — they're broad-based, and could have their members doing all or any of the activities in the following pages. You probably know about some of them, and you can look them up in a telephone book, but it's a handy thing to have them all together.

Scout Association of Ireland, 7 Anglesea Street 2 (711244). Beavers (5-7); Cubs (7-11); Scouts (11-17); Sea and Air Scouts; Handicapped Scouts; Venturers (15-20) / *Catholic Boy Scouts of Ireland,* 19 Herbert Place, 2 (761598). Cubs (8-11); Scouts (11- 15); Venturers (16-19) / *Irish Girl Guides,* 27 Pembroke Park, 4 (683898). Brownies (6-11); Guides (11-16); Land and Sea Rangers (15-21) / *Catholic Girl Guides,* 36 Harrington St., 8 (751774). Brigini (6-8); Guides (9+) / *Girls Brigade,* 5 Upper Sherrard Street, 1 (365488). Explorers (5-8); Juniors (9-12); Seniors (12-14); Brigadiers (15+)/ *Boys Brigade,* 8 Dawson Street, 2 (791857). Anchor Boys (5-8); Juniors (9-12); Company (12-17) / *An Oige, Irish Youth Hostel Organisation,* 39 Mountjoy Square, 1 (363111). There are fifty hostels around the country which provide cheap, clean accommodation, and there are also cycling and adventure sports. You can stay in cheap-rated hostels worldwide / *USIT, Union of Students in Ireland,* 19 Aston Quay, 2 (778117). They issue student travel discount cards, and have cheap travel deals themselves. For school and third-level students / *National Youth Council,* 3 Montague Street, 4 (784122). / *National Youth Federation,* 2 Belvedere Place, 1, (729933) / *Catholic Youth Council,* 20-23 Arran Quay, 7 (725055). Organiser of Catholic youth clubs, and non-denominational Summer Projects / *Church of Ireland Youth Council,* 74 Upper Leeson Street, 2 (607122). Organiser of C of I youth clubs /*Dublin Corporation Youth Information Centre,* Sackville Place, 1 (786844). Open weekdays and Saturdays. Information on sports clubs, jobs, grants etc. Youth literature and videos for consultation / *Slogadh,* 26 Merrion Square, 2 (767283) / *Community Games,* 22 Store St. 1 (788095). There is a youth branch of *Amnesty International,* who campaign for human rights all over the world. Young people's work in this area is very valuable. Information from *Amnesty International,* 8 Shaw Street, 2 (776361) / If you have grandparents or perhaps even great-grandparents you'll know how much they like to see you. *Friends of the Elderly* is an organisation which brings company and activity to older people — teenagers are very welcome. Their office is at 25 Bolton Street, 1 (731855).

The Irish Youth Directory contains a full list of all other youth organisations, left out here because they apply more to groups than to individuals. Published by and available from The National Youth Council of Ireland, 3 Montague Street, 2.

FIRST AID

St John's Ambulance Brigade, 29 Upper Leeson St., 2 (688077) / Order of Malta Ambulance Corps, 32 Clyde Road, 4 (684891). Both offer simple first aid classes in various locations, or you can decide to join the Brigade/Corps later on. That gets you to concerts, matches, big events as a bonus.

HOBBIES AND SKILLS

Archaeology

For a taste of how our very ancient forefathers lived, ate, slept and celebrated, and all the detective work involved in finding these matters out, you could join the Irish Young Archaeologists. It's open to anyone aged between 9 and 18. There are meetings in the National Museum annex in Merrion Row about 6 times a year, some outings and a members' newsletter. Contact Patricia Ryan at 533158.

Astronomy

Astronomy Ireland have a youth group, a newsletter for members, and star-gazing nights for the general public (advertised in the papers). They run a telephone hotline, and sometimes a seasonal 'Space Camp' for young members (residential) and participate in the RDS Youth Science and Arts Week. Send a SAE to PO Box 2888, Dublin 1, for details. See how to get into Dunsink Observatory in Inside Jobs chapter. (page 102)

Computers
Some schools have excellent users' clubs. The Virgin Games Shop in Dawson Street and the games section of their Megastore on Burgh Quay carry notices for games enthusiasts. Apple Mackintosh users can contact Clubmac at 68B Serpentine Avenue, 4 (687191). Amiga users can try NAG — Northside Amiga Group (8401374).

Cookery
You can learn to cook from a book or from the cook in your family. But learning the clever tricks can be fun, and there are several summer courses to set you off on the cordon bleu trail. The Busy Bee Summer School of Cookery is at 2A St Patrick's Avenue, Dalkey (2858728) — 2-week courses for the 11-17-age-group/Teenage Practical Cookery School is at 5 Wilderwood Grove, Templeogue, 6W (552238) 1-week courses for 12-15-year-olds / Alix Gardner Cookery School is at Kensington Hall, Lower Rathmines Road, 6 (960045) — 1-week courses during July and August for 10-15-year-olds.

Design
Art classes are a help if you are interested in dress design. Grafton Academy of Dress Design run a summer course for interested teenagers. They're at 6 Herbert Place, Dublin 2 (767940).

Model Railways
The Model Railway Society of Ireland is northside-based — (378680) / The South Dublin Model Railway Club can be written to at the Gate Lodge, Simpson's Hospital, Ballinteer, 16 / Mark's Models shop in Hawkins Street can answer queries about regular fixtures among model train people.

Model Car Racing
Come to Belfield car park (beside the Science block) on fine Sundays at noon to see the racing of radio-controlled cars. If you or any of the family are bitten by the bug any of the racers will give you news of club events. (See page 91)

Photography
An Oige Photography Club, Mountjoy Square, 1 (363111) takes members of all age groups and trains in developing and printing. Many youth clubs have photography groups. There are classes in almost all community schools and the VEC run classes too.

Stamps
An Post's Philatelic Service runs the Voyager Club for young stamp enthusiasts. They're based at the GPO (Room 2322) and you can write in or call in for details. Otherwise contact Commandant P. Casey, Officers' Quarters, Cathal Brugha Barracks, 6, of the Federation of Philatelic Societies of Ireland, for addresses of local junior clubs.

Steam Railways/Train Spotting
Train spotters and steam maniacs can join either (a) The Irish Railway Record Society, who actually hold their meetings in Heuston Station, 8 (you can write to them there for details), or (b) The Railway Preservation Society of Ireland, who organise actual steam train outings, several per year, open to everyone. Contact Barry Carse, 2 Oakley Square, 6.

Wargames
For wargames of the strictly military and historical kind, Wild Geese Club meet in Rathmines regularly. Contact Robert McClean at 11 Cypress Road, Mount Merrion, Co Dublin (2888691). Dungeons and dragons types should betake themselves to the Virgin games stores in Dawson Street and Burgh Quay for news of happenings in fantasy games. Two regular events are Gaelcon and Leprecon (usually October and January, respectively) and you can ask in the shops about these massive moots of fantasy gamers.

MONEY AND GLORY OR WORK AND WORK

By law you should be 14 to get a part-time job, so don't say I didn't tell you. At ages in or around that the easiest jobs to come by are: babysitting, cleaning, shop assisting, lounge bar work. The way to get them is by asking around, i.e. togged out in your best, go into pubs and shops and ask. Small local shops often have ads in their windows for cleaners and baby-sitters: you can also put one in yourself advertising your services.

If you have particular interests like animals or motor bikes/cars, you should try to get a job you'd enjoy. When you're known at a garage or stables/kennels, obviously it's all that much easier. But there is always the Golden Pages — get the addresses, write rather than phone, in short, neat letters. The Zoo's Pets' Corner, for instance, takes helpers in the summer, but you can imagine what a plum job that is. (Best way is to join the Zoo first, see Chapter 6).

Some people make a lot of commission selling lines: you need to be charming or be cheeky. Ask the next person you see doing it — it'll be a start / Run your own Sales of Work — for profit or for charity, but say which. Tables will do for stalls if it's to be in the garden. Food can be made, while books, comics, records will sell quickly if they're cheap. You can have extra attractions — I used to charge 1d. to shake hands with our cat — a talented animal! / Deliver local newspapers — the free ones. They need quick, efficient delivery persons. Write to or phone the distribution department of your local paper / If you are photogenic you could be a model. The Nan Morgan Agency, 13 Herbert Place (766625) takes all ages on their books. You need to send photographs and proof of parent's permission.

If you are 15 plus, you are the legal school-leaving age, so you could register with FAS, who operate a Youthreach scheme. Head office is 27 Upper Baggot Street, 4 (685777) or try any local branch listed in the phone directory. They have temporary and permanent jobs and will tell you about training / If you fancy a job (temporary) as Assistant Playground Leader, those jobs are advertised in all the national papers in May / The Department of Education, Marlborough Street, will let you have details of EEC and Arts Council grants for music and art.

Getting published, publicised or broadcast

It's so nice to see your name in print that lots of people will write for nothing. Even writing a letter to the Letters Page of a newspaper is exciting. You can write to any paper or magazine with an article or letter, and why not.

Write clearly so that the sub-editor can put printing directions. If you can, get it typed, and leave a lot of space between lines. If you want it back, send a stamped addressed envelope with it. Here are some of the outlets who are interested in young people's work: The *Evening Herald* has a youth page every Saturday / The *Irish Press* has a children's page every Saturday also and the *Evening Press,* on Saturdays, has Junior Press. Letters, opinions and fights! / The *RTE Guide* has a Kidstuff page with occasional competitions and letter pages / Local associations often publish their own newsletters: you'll know if there is one in your district. The free suburban newspapers will also be delighted if you have anything to say. Write to the Editor. If you join a club that has a newsletter or magazine you can write for it and perhaps get involved in the editorial work — this is valuable experience for any would-be writer.

Getting broadcast is not as easy because it's that much more glamorous. But have a bash. There's RTE Radio 1, 2FM and a host of other radio stations in the Dublin catchment area. The popular music shows have requests, quizzes, phone-ins — it just takes a lot of patience to get through on the phone. RTE 1 television and 2FM have a number of young people's programmes, clubs, music, discussions. If you want to get involved, write in to the producer (listen at the end of the programme, or look his or her name up in the *RTE Guide*), and explain what you'd like to say on the air.

If you are doing anything unusual as a hobby, or in a group, or as a sports club, you've nothing to lose. And they have competitions too. Remember: the address you need is the producer's name, the programme, RTE, Dublin 4.

SPORTS

You will not find one word about most common school sports below — if they are your passion, you already know how to follow them up. No — this is a connoisseur's list so don't just skip it because you ain't the sporty type. Some of these are exciting spectator sports that would make a great family outing — others are all action. I have divided sports into categories of my own that would probably put the Olympic Council into paroxysms of laughter, but to me they seem highly efficient.

ADVENTURE SPORTS

You will need the following addresses for many of the sports listed in the following pages. They specialise in what is known as 'adventure sports' — which is, basically, outdoor, non-competitive, except for yourself against the elements, exciting sport.

AFAS, the Association for Adventure Sports has an office at House of Sport, Long Mile Road, 12 (509845). The National Adventure Centre at: Tiglin Adventure Centre, Ashford, Co. Wicklow (0404) 40169. For groups and individuals, but booking is essential. Canoeing, all sorts, river trekking, rock climbing, navigation, walking in all terrain, orienteering, caving, hang-gliding, wind-surfing, mapmaking and snorkelling / An Oige, 39 Mountjoy Square (363111). Takes groups and individual members hiking, climbing, pony-trekking, cycling, canoeing, swimming and mountaineering.

Whew! But they're cheap, and you meet people too!

Lakeside Leisure, Burgage, Blessington, Co Wicklow (054-65092) is a multi-activity centre on the lake, open to families, schools and groups of all kinds. You can drop in, but at weekends it is advisable to book, and you can check out what clothing and/or equipment you will need. On offer are: canoeing, windsurfing, sailing, pony trekking, tennis, orienteering, abseiling and archery. There's a restaurant and in the summer a 12-seater Galway hooker cruises on the lake.

Skirmish is a 'woodland' game, really a tactical war game, in which two teams establish camps and try to steal each other's flags. *Gauntlet* is an assault and obstacle course with three different levels of difficulty. Over 10s can take part in both, and birthday parties are also catered for. The base is the Glenview Hotel, Glen O' the Downs, Co Wicklow where you ask for Skirmish (Ireland) Ltd (2873399).

AIR SPORTS

Flying — Irish Aero Club, Iona Hangar, Cloghran, Co. Dublin (375228) — take the back road to the airport, via Ballymun. 16 is the required age to gain a solo licence. It's a very expensive sport, but plane-spotting is free, here and at Weston Aerodrome near Celbridge. Passengers can take half-hour sight-seeing trips, also expensive, and there are short trial lessons at a much reduced rate. For Air Displays see calendar, page xx.

Gliding — Dublin Gliding Club, $^c/_o$ D. Begley, 1 Oakdown Road, 14 (2983994). Pilots meet at Gowrangrange, off the Punchestown Road, 3 miles past Naas, on Saturdays and Sundays. Licence is for over 16s, but, at discretion, younger people can take lessons. For passengers, there's no age limit and it's possible to get a trial membership to try it out.

Para-gliding / Hang-gliding — Hang-gliding & Para-gliding Centre, 16 Mask Road, Artane, 5 (314551). There are summer courses for over 16s, and weekend courses at Easter, based in the Wicklow mountains. As well as practical gliding techniques, students learn meteorology, navigation and rules of the air. Spectators should climb the Sugarloaf mountain for a close look at the magnificent people.

Note: all air sports are necessarily expensive because of intensive training, high-tech equipment and insurance cover.

WATER SPORTS

Angling — Dodder Anglers' Club, $^c/_o$ R. O'Hanlon, 82 Braemor Road, Churchtown, 14 (2982112), has many young members, and runs courses in winter on the basics of angling. There are also winter classes in several vocational schools: ring the VEC, Town Hall, Ballsbridge (680614), for details / Some youth clubs have angling groups. Enquire at your local club.

Canoeing — The Irish Canoe Union, House of Sport, Long Mile Road, 12 (509838) has details of local clubs and courses of all kinds. / See AFAS and An Oige listings in this chapter.

SHOULD HAVE
N THE ONE
AT GOT AWAY.
WAS THIS BIG!

Rowing — Dublin Municipal Rowing Centre at Islandbridge on the Liffey is for school groups and youth clubs. It's got excellent facilities and is run by the Corporation (779746) / The Irish Amateur Rowing Union, House of Sport, Long Mile Road, 12 (509838) / Sea Scouts teach rowing, and rowing boats can be hired in several places like Dalkey and Rush, if there's an experienced oarsperson along.

Sailing — Fingall Sailing School, Malahide (8451979) teaches sailing in small boats to over 10s, according to Irish Yachting Association rules/So does the Irish National Sailing School, 115 Lower George's Street, Dun Laoghaire (2806654) or contact Irish Yachting Association (2800239) for details of local clubs and courses / You can take sailing as an option at the Blessington Lakes Leisure Pursuits Centre — see above, and with AFAS. Sea Scouts excel at sailing (see youth organisations) and Glenans Irish Sailing Club, 28 Merrion Square 2 (611481) organise cheap residential sailing courses for families and over/Coiste an Asgard — Asgard 11 is Ireland's first sail training ship and it gives exciting sea-faring experiences to accepted applicants, over the age of 15, male and female. Write or phone for details to Coiste an Asgard, Infirmary Road, 8 (6792169).

Swimming — The most basic water sport of all, and suitable for anyone over three months of age. There is a list of the various kinds of pools at the end of this chapter. Lessons in swimming and water safety are available in most pools, at various times — ring the local pool for details. Also contact the Irish Amateur Swimming Association, House of Sport, Long Mile Road, 12 (501739) for details of clubs and intensive training.

Wind-surfing — Surfdock (683945) in Grand Canal Dock, Fingall Sailing and Windsurfing School (8451979) Wind and Wave Windsurfing, 16A The Crescent, Monkstown (2844177) all offer junior rigs and specialised training. You can also take windsurfing as an option in adventure sports centres like AFAS and Blessington Lakes Leisure Pursuits.

Life-saving and Water-safety — Contact the National Safety Council, 4 Northbrook Road, 6 (963422) for details of classes held in local pools. Certificates are awarded.

General — You can do watery sporty things right in the heart of Dublin at Surf Dock, The Grand Canal Dock, South Dock Road, Ringsend, 4 (683945). There are one-day 'taster' events and other packages of canoeing/windsurfing for schools, plus individual classes in both, and an introduction to scuba diving (for the latter 12-16s need a parent present in the water; over 16s need written consent). There's even a drydock high wind simulator for advanced surfers! Junior windsurfing classes happen during summer months for 8-14-year-olds. Junior rigs and wetsuits available.

MOTOR AND MACHINE SPORTS

Cycling — As a sport rather than a means of getting from here to there, cycling is divided into touring and racing. Many youth clubs take touring trips. A bike needs to be well maintained for both categories — get yours checked by an expert. **Touring:** An Oige Cycling Club (363111) / Cyclists Touring Club, c/o John Bailey, 123 Roselawn Road, 15 (8201871). Families and young people welcome on weekend trips of Dublin and bordering counties, back same day / Dublin Roadsters Cycling Club. Similar, and meets on Sundays at 10.30 am at Harold's Cross Bridge on the Grand Canal / Little Sports Cycling Club is especially for young people and was started by the pioneering Eamonn Duffy, who owns the Little Sports shop in Fairview (332405). Meet on Sundays at 11.00 am at the Little Sports shop in Fairview. **Racing** — Contact the Federation of Irish Cyclists, Halston Street, 7 (727524). For the National School-boy/girl Cycling Championships see Calendar, Chapter 12. **Bicycle Polo** — On view every Sunday at 11.00 am in the polo grounds of the Phoenix Park. It's like trick cycling and is very skilled. **Go-Karting** — On the Swords

Road, just before the old Collinstown road to the airport, there's a sign and a rutty path that leads to the Go-Kart track. It's open from 10.00 am to 11.00 pm in summer. You must be over 13, and follow the track rules. Helmets provided, and the charge depends on the number of laps. Best done in company of friends.

Karting and Stock-car racing: On view at Mondello Park, Naas, Co. Kildare, (045 60200) and on Sundays at Santry Stockcar Track.

Road Safety — There is a Traffic Education School in Clontarf, which is great fun for a day. There are film shows and then you're out on the miniature road system, double yellow lines and all, as pedestrians, cyclists (bikes available) and motorists (pedal cars available). It's run by Dublin Corporation mainly through schools, but also for scouts and summer project groups. Contact the Road Safety Unit of the Corporation (6796111 — ext 2504).

LAND SPORTS

Archery — Irish Amateur Archery Federation, $^c/_o$ James Conroy, 103 St Brendan's Avenue, 5 (8481574). Five clubs in Dublin. Children and families especially welcome. Some adventure centres offer archery as an option, and there is an archery club and centre at the Glenview Hotel, Glen O'the Downs, Co Wicklow (2873399).

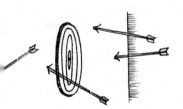 

Caving — AFAS. Do *not* go caving anywhere without skilled company.

Walking/Hiking — AFAS / An Oige / Dublin Walking Club, $^c/_o$ Geraldine Byrne, 61 Ardcollum Avenue, 5 (8474578). Welcomes families and young people. Every June International Walk standard medals are awarded.

Mountaineering — AFAS / An Oige.

Tennis — There is a list of public tennis courts at the end of this book. You can enquire at your local court about classes. But the best organised scheme for young people is the Dublin Parks Tennis League, which operates three seasons of the year in 54 centres throughout the city. Registration is very cheap, and if you don't have the gear, racquets and balls are provided. Thousands of young people are interested but the scheme is very successfully keeping pace and there are inter-city matches. For those over 16, FAS run a tennis coaching scheme in conjunction with the DPTL. For information contact Kay Lonergan (338711).

Apart from this excellent public scheme there are literally dozens of private tennis clubs in Dublin — if you don't know of one consult the Golden Pages! Lots of sports centres offer special indoor coaching — make enquiries. Several summer camps offer intensive coaching.

INDOOR SPORTS

Boxing — Nearly all big youth clubs teach boxing. For more specialised training contact: Irish Amateur Boxing Association, $^c/_o$ National Stadium, South Circular Road, 8 (533371).

Fencing — Salle d'Armes, St John's Road, Sandymount, 4 (2693720). This is a fencing school, and there are classes for children during term as well as holidays. There are weekend courses for slightly older age-groups, as trial runs before getting into the equipment-stage.

Bowling — There are bowling centres in Stillorgan (2881656); Crumlin (555659); Dundrum (2980209); Tallaght (599411); North Strand Road (741868). Booking a lane in advance is strongly advised unless you just want to hang out among the video games.

Laser adventure games — not exactly a sport but great fun. They're to be found alongside the bowling at Tallaght, Dundrum and North Strand. Special party deals complete with meal — enquiries from the numbers above.

Gymnastics — Irish Amateur Gymnastics Association, House of Sport, Long Mile Road, 12 (501805). Most clubs take members aged 6 and over. There are local clubs all over the city and the sport is really taking off.

Karate — Classes all over. Contact the Official Amateur Karate Association of Ireland (James Booth at 744835/726922) for approved classes for young people and details of championships. The Irish Kenpo Karate Union also has clubs all over the city and young members are very welcome. Contact Paul Brennan (311743).

Judo — Contact the Irish Judo Association, 79 Upper Dorset Street, 1 (302607) for local classes and clubs.

Table-Tennis — Facilities at all youth clubs, sports centres and community schools. For information about tournaments contact: Irish Table-Tennis Association, $^c/_o$ T. Martin, 46 Lorcan Villas, Santry, 9 (8421679).

Ice-Skating — Dublin Ice Rink, Dolphin's Barn (532170). Open for three sessions, morning, afternoon, evening. Check times. The rink is realistically cold so bring gloves and warm clothes. The skates are good, but if you have your own, admission is much cheaper. Group and private classes are available and initiates can play ice hockey at times — that is what the strange markings are for. For starters and shaky leggers there's the ice, disco music and refreshments. Accessories are for sale in the Skate Shop.

Snooker — Press your waistcoat and polish your shades — you could be on telly along with the best of them. Seriously, if you are interested you already know your local pool hall, or table, and the rules of the place. 16 is the age for playing League games. But the bigger centres often run Junior League from about 12 upwards. Queries to the Republic of Ireland Billiards and Snooker Association, $^c/_o$ Dermot Dalton, House of Sport, Long Mile Road, 12 (509850).

There are many local purpose-built sports centres with a huge menu of indoor sports to choose from, as well as facilities in community schools — check sports clubs in the Golden Pages. Dublin Corporation have a large sports complex in Aughrim Street (388085) used by many youth groups.

ANIMAL SPORTS

Horse-riding — There is a list of riding schools at the end of the book. The Irish Pony Club is a youth organisation for under-17s interested in horses and riding. They hold rallies during school holidays and lectures, films and instruction all year round. They say 'possession of a pony is desirable but not essential'. For details of branches (nearly all affiliated to local hunts) and membership fees contact: Mrs. P. Riall, Knocbawn, Rocky Valley Drive, Kilmacanogue, Co. Wicklow (2863543). Pony-trekking is an option at the Blessington Lakes Leisure Pursuits Centre (045-65092).

Horse-racing — The race-course near Dublin is Leopardstown — lots of buzz and a great day out for everyone. There are special buses that go further afield to Punchestown, the Curragh and Fairyhouse, leaving from Busarus. Look up the papers for fixtures. Officially you cannot bet until you are 18 but an obliging adult can help you exercise your flutter. There are admission charges to enclosures but you can watch the race and the crazy-looking tote from outside.

Harness and Trot Racing — Portmarnock Raceway, every Sunday at 3.30 pm (from April to October). Tel 8462834. Another good day out. Car park free with admission charge, and children very reasonable. It's a very Kentuckyish sport.

Polo — In the Phoenix Park, weekend afternoons from May to September. Free to watch. The polo ponies are small, skinny and swift, a breed apart.

Pigeons — A big Dublin sport is racing pigeons, and there are pigeons in a lot of backyards. If they're in yours you probably know all about it, but if you want to know more contact the Dublin Homing Pigeon Club, 2 Shaun Terrace, 3 (741960).

Dogs — Racing, Training and Showing are not for your family dog maybe, but you never know. *Racing* — Not as glamorous as horse-racing, but still a good night out. There are two stadiums in Dublin: Shelbourne Park, on Mondays, Wednesdays and Saturdays; Harold's Cross, Tuesdays, Thursdays and Fridays. All meetings at 8.00 pm. *Training* — There are several centres for obedience training, if you can't manage it on your own. Contact the Mansize Dog Training

School, Swords, Co. Dublin for details of local venues. *Showing* — usually means pedigree dogs, but small local shows often have 'all comers' class. Several of the larger shows also have a children's showing class — otherwise there's no age-limits (for the showers!) Contact the Irish Kennel Club, Unit 36, Greenmount Office Park, Dublin 6 (533300).

Cats — About shows and showing, contact the Siamese and All Breeds Cat Club (972783).

The Zoo — Finally, why not join the Zoo? Membership goes towards animal maintenance. Contact The Royal Zoological Society of Ireland, Phoenix Park, 8 (771425).

WINTER SPORTS

Skiing — No, not the real thing, though you can ski in nearby Scotland. But the Ski Club of Ireland have classes on the artificial slope at the Kilternan Sports Hotel (2955658) beginning in autumn.

Sledging — Probably no-one needs to be told but there are some great slopes in the Dublin mountains, especially near the Pine Forest. Any slope will do with the right coverage and toy and sports shops stock cheap plastic sledges as well as the fancy ones with runners.

Ice-skating — see indoor sports: it's all year round!

WILD LIFE and ENVIRONMENT

Some of these societies are nature-spotting — others are more involved with conservation. Either way you get out and about, and in winter get a real kick out of wild life television programmes.

Irish Wildbird Conservancy organises regular local outings, lectures and activities and has a newsletter, posters and stationery. Families and young people welcome with appropriate discounts. Contact IWC, Ruttledge House, 8 Longford Place, Monkstown, Co. Dublin (2804322) / An Oige (363111) organises natural history walks and lectures / The Dublin Naturalists Field Club, $^c/_o$ St Martin's House, Waterloo Road, 4, takes members on regular fascinating trips connected with every imaginable aspect of wild life. Night lectures also / ECO — Irish Environmental Conservation Organisation for Youth, 11 Cope Street, 2 (6799673) organises workshops and practical education for individuals and groups. They also run summer camps. Aimed at over 15s but they can work with schools / An Taisce, Tailors Hall, Back Lane, 8, (541786) nationwide conservation organisation, with mainly adult membership but family membership is worth considering because of the broad range of activities and interests (and magazine) / Coillte, Leeson Lane, 2 (615666). A semi-state department concerned with forestry. They send out literature and forestry careers information to all inquirers. / Crann, Aughavas, via Cavan, Co. Leitrim (078-36020). An organisation that promotes afforestation and gives advice to all kinds of tree lovers and growers. Very helpful for school projects, has family membership and a regular newsletter / The Wildlife Service, $^c/_o$ 51 St Stephen's Green, 2 (613111). A government department that answers queries about protected species, and works through the National Parks and Monuments Service — useful for project work / ENFO — Environmental Information Service, 17 St Andrew Street, 2 (6793144). A walk-in centre with great facilities (see Inside Jobs) / Greenpeace, 44 Upper Mount Street, 2 (619836) does trojan and often dangerous work throughout the world in protecting the planet from the worst human excesses. Has a newsletter with a children's page, and offers family membership. Finally, two out-of-the-country organisations specially geared to young people and supplying attractive literature to members: Gerald Durrell's Dodo Club, $^c/_o$ Jersey Wildlife Preservation Trust, Les Augres Manor, Jersey, Channel Islands. Not in Dublin, but most of its members are not in Jersey either. Designed specifically for young people who are interested in saving rare species — hence the name. You get a badge and the excellent Dodo Dispatch newspaper which has full colour posters. Membership fee is in sterling so write for exact details / Young Ornithologists Club — junior branch of the Royal Society for the Protection of Birds — produces an excellent magazine for young members. For membership details write to: Young Ornithologists Club, RSPB, The Lodge, Sandy, Bedfordshire, SG19 2DL.

Chapter 10
STILL BORED?

YEH!

This is a list of items *not* covered in this book, but there is no reason why *you* shouldn't do a pioneering job.

Follow a ghost railway line before it becomes alive again! It's planned to rebuild the Harcourt line as a busway or light railway. It's on maps of Dublin before 1957. It's got some magnificent viaducts and several ghost stations.

Organise a tiphead outing with gang or family: Dump your unwanteds and look around for bargains. People throw away the most enticing articles, and you'll always get a good selection of wheels. Go carefully! List of tips in the telephone book under Dublin Corporation and County Council.

See if your family is interested in *renting a strip of bog* to dig, in the mountains. You can call it your country estate. Details from Dublin and Wicklow county councils.

Go *plane-spotting* on the back road behind Dublin airport — past Ballymun to Cloghran — the runways end just here.

Climb the Sugarloaf mountain.

Find statues of monkeys at mischief in Kildare Street.

Explore a wasteland and see how many rare plants and flowers you can find and identify. Even city centre patches can have botanical marvels. (Use a pocket guide like *Collins' Gem Guide to Wild Flowers.*)

Photograph old shopfronts — they might disappear before you next pass by.

Go on overnight camp with your family far from civilisation, or even a regular site. Consult a camping equipment shop — it's possible to rent everything!

Find a blueberry (frauchan) patch in the Dublin mountains and have the berries on your cereal.

Find out one *thing about Dublin* that only *you* know but that you don't mind sharing, and write to me care of Wolfhound Press, Mountjoy Square, 1. It will get into the next edition, with your name as discoverer, as long as it's not criminal!

Chapter 11
GET OUT!

A short-list of day trips out of Dublin. Some require planning and an entire day — they're well worth it!

Charter an historic sea voyage in a Galway Hooker, or if you have a group of 20, travel as Vikings in the Dyflin longboat! Both vessels operate from the Liffey near Grand Canal Dock. The *Cliona na Toinne* hooker gives short day cruises, and longer weekend ones, like a sail up to the Boyne (Drogheda), going on to the great archaeological remains by bike (see below). Both hooker and longboat trips are by mutual agreement. Contact: Barry Jones or John Burns at 62/64 Fenian Street, 2 (764942/683634).

Avondale Forest Park, Rathdrum, Co. Wicklow. Car or train (but there's quite a walk). The home of Charles Stewart Parnell, whose ancestors had a passion for exotic trees. Avondale is now the forestry service school and there are all sorts of timber and nature trails.

The Japanese Gardens, Tully, Co. Kildare (045-21617). Car. Here the Willow Pattern teaset design comes to life. Bridges and bonsai trees and glorious cherry blossom in late Spring. Could combine with:

The National Stud, Kildare (045-21617). Thoroughbreds, jockeys and all that business. Wonderhorse Arkle has his skeleton preserved in the museum.

Newgrange Burial Chamber and Newgrange Farm, near Slane, Co. Meath. Car. Bus tour from Busarus during the summer. Stretched along the river Boyne (you should also take in the Battle of 1690 site near Drogheda) are a series of wondrous megalithic burial chambers. Some are still being excavated. Newgrange spooks adults more than children because of its narrow entrance and 5000-year-old passages

— older than the Pyramids. Beside it is Newgrange Farm, a working farm with lots of animals and birds to meet and a great coffee shop.

Glendalough, Co Wicklow. Car or the St Kevin's Bus (11.30 am from the Royal College of Surgeons, St Stephen's Green). Two spooky lakes, oak forest, round tower and ancient churches. Good picnicking.

Laytown Races, Laytown, Co. Meath. Car or train from Connolly. Horse-racing on Laytown beach happens every year in August; the date is set entirely according to the spring tides, and is advertised in the press. A great spectacle, with tidal waves of atmosphere. Good swimming on Bettystown beach further down. Dunes and a funfair.

Fun Tropica, Mosney, Co Meath. Car or train from Connolly. Day tickets for the holiday camp allow full participation in the waterworld and carnival amusements. Indoor and outdoor heated pools — the indoor one has the slides, jacuzzi and sprays. Burgers and snack food available, or you can bring a picnic.

Irish National Heritage Park, Ferrycarrig, Co Wexford (053-41733). Car. It's an 'ideal homes' exhibition, only the homes go back through 9,000 years. Hunter/gatherers had homesteads too, and there's a livable reconstruction here of a mesolithic camp-site by water. Crannogs, neolithic farms, stone circles, ringforts, a Crusader-like castle and early industry and crafts are on display in this attractive wooded park just outside Wexford town.

Celtworld, Tramore, Co. Waterford. Bus or car. Celtworld offers a fantasy trip back to Druidic times and the adventures of Celtic heroes. A crystalline Time Chamber does the trick — helped a little by lasers and holograms and other brand-new computer tricks. You can choose to be at home in the Otherworld or among the Fianna and after the trip Tramore has lots of traditional seaside activities and new developments. (051-81330)

Kilkenny City. Car or train. Walk about the Castle and the river, don't miss Cityscope in the Almshouse (and tourist information centre) — it's a sound and light exhibition of a miniature Kilkenny city as it was in its glory days of 1642. In summer there's a special bus trip (or take car on the Castlecomer road) to stalagtite/mite-rich Dunmore Caves (056-22036 for information).

Clara Bog Train trip. Also called the Clonmacnois and West Offaly Railway. Car to Athlone, take road to Clonmacnois, stopping at this beautiful Shannonside monastic site, and on to Shannonbridge where the train is signposted. It's a 45-minute trip through industrial bog, flower and wildlife bog and historical bog. (For dates and times: 0905-74114)

Armagh Planetarium. Car or bus from Busarus. Just outside Armagh city. Daytrips on Saturdays take in the starshows (2.00 pm and 3.00 pm) and the Hall of Astronomy which offers Encyclopedia Galactica on 12 different computer terminals. Visitors can sit at the controls of one of the world's largest telescopes. There's a space shop. (Armagh: 0861-523689).

Ulster Folk and Transport Museum, Cultra, Co Down. Car or train and bus. A shopping person could be deposited in Belfast to be picked up later while the rest of the family go here — it's only a short way out of the city. There's a recreated pre-Famine village with all the crafts of home and farm, and beautiful houses, some rebuilt stone by stone here. And buses, tractors, engines of all sorts. Carriage rides available in summer. (084-428428).

Take a day trip with Iarnrod Eireann on one of their special value KID tickets (one or two adults, up to four children). You can go to places like Fota Wildlife Park in Cork, take a Lough Corrib cruise, the Giant's Causeway, a river cruise in Waterford or the Ulster Folk and Transport Museum as above. Ask Iarnrod Eireann for booking details (366222).

Go to *Wales or Roman England* at Chester. Sealink Stena Line have very reasonably priced day trips from Dun Laoghaire to Holyhead (you're gone from 9.00 am to 6.00 pm) or further into Wales/England, taking the London train as far as Bangor, Llandudno or Chester (you go at 9.00 am and are back in Dun Laoghaire at 5.30 am next morning). These trips do not operate all the year around: make enquiries at 2808844.

Or very simply — why not take a DART round trip — Howth and Bray in one day? Special family tickets available.

Chapter 12
CALENDAR

This calendar lists a selection of regular annual events of special appeal. Most, like Easter, are movable feasts — so for exact dates you have to watch out for publicity, or contact the organisation concerned. And it doesn't pretend to be an exhaustive list — but it might fill some holes in the family calendar.

JANUARY
FUNDERLAND at the RDS Extension, Ballsbridge. Usually lasts a month from St Stephen's Day. Biggest fun-fair in Ireland / Aer Lingus YOUNG SCIENTISTS Exhibition, first/second weeks. In the RDS Main Hall, Ballsbridge / PAINT-IN sessions for children, National Gallery of Ireland, Merrion Square, during the holidays. Supervised by artists.

FEBRUARY
International BOAT SHOW, RDS, mid-February or March / All- Ireland IRISH DANCING Championships, Mansion House /AER RIANTA ARTS FESTIVAL, DUBLIN AIRPORT — something for everyone.

MARCH
St Patrick's Day PARADE, 17th March from St Stephen's Green to the GPO. (Tip — arrive early and wander around the assembly point — St Stephen's Green itself — for an exciting close-up of the floats and bands) / DOG SHOW in the RDS, 17th March / Irish MOTOR SHOW, every second year at the RDS Extension /MIGRATION WATCH, phone Irish Wildbird Conservancy (2804322) for details / Outside Dublin — March/April, Easter Bunny STEAM TRAIN run from Mullingar, details from Railway Preservation Society of Ireland (page 134).

APRIL

First CUCKOO / FEIS MAITIU, Father Matthew Hall, Church St., 7 — Irish music and dancing competitions / Tailteann SWIMMING Championship. Contact Irish Amateur Swimming Association / Combined Canine Club DOG SHOW, RDS, Easter Sunday / CIRCUIT OF IRELAND RALLY — Easter Weekend.

MAY

Punchestown RACES, 3-day Special Event / SPRING SHOW, RDS. First week. Biggest pigs, hugest bulls, cleverest dogs, most gorgeous horses. And freebies of all kinds / FEIS CEOIL, competitions and concerts. Mid-May. Various venues /National BIKE DAY, a Sunday in late May. Rallies for everyone. Contact Cospoir / National SPORT FOR ALL Day. First Sunday in the month. Various venues and events. Contact Cospoir / LIBERTIES FESTIVAL, April /May. Many outdoor events.

JUNE

National CHILDREN'S DAY. Sunday early in June. Parade through Dublin / International 2-DAY WALKS, a weekend in June. Different length walks all Northside. Contact Dublin Walking Club / Veteran and Vintage CAR RALLY, mid-June. Starts from Donnybrook / MODEL AERONAUTIC Championships, (usually) Blackrock College, Co. Dublin / Dun Laoghaire SUMMER FESTIVAL. Various venues in Dun Laoghaire. / MALAHIDE Festival, Malahide Castle Grounds / MARACYCLE — Dublin-Belfast / DUBLIN STREET CARNIVAL — crazy fun, theatre, clowns, music. Free and otherwise.

JULY

Summer PROJECTS begin / JUNIOR TRACK Championships, Santry / Irish VETERAN and VINTAGE International Race, from Dublin to Athy / Glencullen FRAUCHAN FESTIVAL, Glencullen, Co. Dublin. (Frauchans are small blueberries). Local Festival with everything from poker to baby shows. / Free POP CONCERTS in Parks. Start now / FUN FAIR, Booterstown Common / Youth SCIENCE Week, RDS. Tel. 680645.

AUGUST

Dublin HORSE SHOW, RDS, first week. All sorts of horses and prestigious jumping events. Also International Folk Dance Festival, arts and crafts, and other displays / AIR SPECTACULAR, Ireland's biggest air display, Fairyhouse Racecourse, Co. Meath. (Contact Aer Rianta) / International GRAND PRIX Races, Phoenix Park / Carroll's Irish Open GOLF CHAMPIONSHIP, Royal Dublin, Dollymount. International golf and a picnic on the beach / Outside Dublin LAYTOWN RACES, Co. Meath. Fantastic BEACH RACES. Spring tide weekend.

SEPTEMBER
COMMUNITY GAMES National Finals Festival, at Butlins Camp, Mosney / International LIFFEY DESCENT. Canoe race from Straffan to Islandbridge. Contact Irish Canoe Union / Forest WALKS. Guided walks in forested areas, nationwide. Second Sunday / GAA FINALS. First and third Sundays, Croke Park.

OCTOBER
Junior Film Festival, Irish Film Centre. / Children's Book Week — actually two weeks / Dublin THEATRE FESTIVAL for 2 weeks — watch out for theatrical events, even though there may not be an official Theatre Festival /National STAMP EXHIBITION at the RDS, Ballsbridge / Fossett's CIRCUS, Booterstown Green — early October for three weeks / Dublin City MARATHON. Come and cheer or even volunteer for face-sponging. Starts 11.00 am Bank Holiday Monday at St Stephen's Green / Blessing of the ANIMALS. You can get your pets large and small blessed at this traditional Dublin ceremony where hens and goldfish turn up alongside their sworn foes. The blessing is at Halston Street Church, near Church Street, just off the quays, and it happens on the second or third Sunday — whichever is nearest the feast of St Francis of Assisi (Oct. 13).

NOVEMBER
Last SWALLOW says goodbye early in the month / Brent GEESE and ARCTIC TERNS say hello / Dublin Indoor International HORSE SHOW mid-month, RDS / Santa CLAUS arrives at pretty well every big store and shopping centre. / Outside Dublin: Santa Claus on a STEAM TRAIN journey from Mullingar. Details from Railway Preservation Society (page 134).

DECEMBER
Mansion House CRIB CONCERT, mid-December / St Patrick's Cathedral CAROL Concert, Christmas Eve. Buy tickets beforehand or go early / PANTOMIMES and children's Christmas drama start St Stephen's Day / Visiting UK or European CIRCUS, Booterstown Green or Whitehall Common, after Christmas / Fancy-dress Moto-cross SCRAMBLE, St Stephen's Day. At Saggart /Rathcoole. Follow the crowd.

Chapter 13

ENTERTAINMENT

Indoor adventure and play centres

Assault courses, slides, ball ponds, bouncing castles, are some of the features of these fun centres, some of which have facilities for up to 13/14 years. All have toddler areas where parents can leave small children because they're completely supervised. Parties are also a speciality (See page 42). Clonsilla: Giraffes, Coolmine Industrial Park (8205526); Coolock: The Zoo, Leisureplex, Malahide Road (8485722); Dundrum: Wally Wabbits, Pye Centre (983470); Dun Laoghaire: The Fun Factory, Monkstown Road (2843344); Santry: Omni Adventure World, Omni Centre (8428844); Stillorgan: Bambams, Kilmacud Road (2884529); Swords: Giraffes, Feltrim Industrial Estate (8408749); Tallaght: Injun Falls, Belgard Road (597440); Captain Venture, The Square (596039)

Circus

The circus season in Dublin is from October till Christmas and after. There are two sites where the circus pitches its Big Top — Booterstown fairground (Buses 6, 7A, 8, 45 from town) and Whitehall, near the Crofton Hotel. (Buses 3, 16, 33 and 41). There are performances nightly and several shows at weekends. Generally Irish circuses perform before Christmas, and a European one performs during the Christmas season. Watch for posters.

Fun-fairs

Apart from Bray (Bus 45) there is no fixed fun-fair in the city, which is a huge pity. Funderland in the RDS, Ballsbridge (Buses 6, 7A, 8, 45) is a huge fair, starting the day after Christmas, for one month. It's got easy rides, thriller rides, sideshows and junk food. Always packed. Booterstown has a summer fun-fair on a much smaller scale — the seaside type, with dodgems and swing-boats. (Buses 6, 7A, 8), June and July.

Puppets
The Lambert Puppet Theatre, Mews, Clifton Lane, Monkstown (2800974), Buses 7A, 8. The full range of puppet technology and magical tales.

FREE ENTERTAINMENT

Free entertainment is reasonably plentiful, but not such a regular thing that it can be faithfully listed. Some ideas to play around with are:

Warships and Sailing Ships
Foreign navies often pay courtesy calls on Dublin port, and their ships and submarines are open to the public, usually weekend afternoons. They are usually moored in (a) Alexandra Basin, North Wall (Bus 53A from Beresford Place, or (b) Dun Laoghaire (Buses 7A, 8, 46A). Watch for sailors around town, or read the What's On columns.

Street Entertainment
Mimes and clowns of varied quality abound in Grafton Street. The Dublin Theatre Festival in October brings over (usually) high-class street theatre.

Park Concerts
St Anne's Park, Blackrock Park, the Phoenix Park have played free rock concerts — you would never miss the publicity. St Stephen's Green has bands, and very occasionally, plays.

Big Store Entertainment
Stores like Switzer's, Arnott's and some shopping centres put on occasional big floor shows — like LegoWorld, and movie spin-offs like Star War Centres. They are good but designed to tempt!

Dublin Corporation Youth Information Centre, Sackville Place (786844) is open on Saturdays as well as weekdays, and the staff are knowledgeable about various happenings, free and otherwise.

For spectacular sports, and other regular fixtures see Chapter 9 and the Calendar.

LIBRARIES

City: Baldoyle 322549 / Ballyfermot 6269325 / Ballymun 8421890 / Central Library 734333 / Charleville Mall, North Strand 749619 / Coolock 8477781 / Dolphin's Barn 540681 / Donaghmede 8482833 / Drumcondra 377206 / Finglas 344906 / Howth 322130 / Inchicore 533793 / Kevin Street 753794 / Marino 336297 / Pearse Street 772764 / Pembroke, Ballsbridge 689575 / Phibsboro 304341 / Raheny 315521 / Rathmines 973539 / Ringsend 680063 / Terenure 907035 /Walkinstown 558159 **County:** Balbriggan 8411128 / Blanchardstown 8212701 / Cabinteely 2855363 / Clondalkin 593315 / Deansgrange 2850860 / Dundrum 2985000 / Malahide 8452026 / Rathbeale 8404179 / Shankill 2823081 / Stillorgan 2889655 / Tallaght 515909.

RIDING SCHOOLS

Ashton Equestrian Centre, Castleknock 387611 / Brennanstown R.S., Kilmacanogue, Co. Wicklow 2863778 / Bridestream Riding Centre, Kilcock 6287261 / Brittas Lodge Stables, Brittas 582162 / Calliaghstown R.C., Rathcoole 589236 / Carrickmines Equestrian Centre, Foxrock, 18, 2955990 / Donacomper R.S., Celbridge 6288221 / Kinsealy R.C., Malahide 8460010 / Kilternan Riding Centre, Kilternan Hotel 2857136 / Malahide R.S. 8463622 / Newcastle R.S., Newcastle 580025 / Riding in Dundrum, 14, 2986112 / Spruce Lodge, Kilternan (also does riding for the disabled) 2952109 / Ryevalley R.C., Leixlip 6244157.

Most riding stables are quite far from the city centre so ask for specific directions.

SWIMMING POOLS

Dublin Corporation Pools *Open Monday-Friday 11.30-3.00, 4.00-8.00; Saturday 10.00-1.00, 2.00-6.00; Sunday 10.00-2.00.* Ballymun Shopping Centre 8421368 / Ballyfermot, Le Fanu Park 6266504 / Coolock Shopping Centre 8477743 / Finglas, Mellowes Road 348005 / Markievicz, Townsend Street 770503 / Rathmines, opp. Town Hall

961275 / Sean McDermott Street 720752 / Willie Pearse Park, Crumlin 555792. **School and other pools open to public:** *Ring for available hours.* CRC, Vernon Avenue, Clontarf 339458 / Coolmine, Clonsilla 214344 / Clondalkin Community Centre 574858 / Dundrum Family Recreation Centre 2984654 / King's Hospital, Palmerstown 6264550 / Marian College, Lansdowne Road, Ballsbridge 689539 / St. Paul's, Raheny 316283 / Portmarnock Sports Centre 8462086 / Templeogue College, Templeville Road 901711/ Terenure College, Templeogue Road 907071.

DUBLIN PUBLIC TENNIS COURTS

Dublin Corporation Parks
Sheriff Street 1, Mountjoy Square 1, Foley Street 1, Pearse Square 2, Ringsend Park 4, Charlemont Street 1, Broadstone, Phibsboro 7, Bridgefoot Street 8, Fatima Mansions, Dolphin House, Rialto 8, St. Theresa's Gardens 8, Basin Lane, Thomas St 8, Ventry Park, Fassaugh Ave., Cabra W. 7, Johnstown Park, Mellowes Road, Finglas 11, Poppintree, Ballymun 11, St. Anne's, Raheny 5, Ellenfield, Whitehall 9, Belcamp, Coolock 5, Albert College, Glasnevin 11, Thorndale, Artane 5, Kilbarrack Community School 3, Donaghmede Park 13, Sundrive Road, Brickfields, Crumlin 12, Bluebell, St. Michael's Estate, Inchicore 8, Walkinstown Park 12, Le Fanu, Ballyfermot 10, Herbert Park 4, Bushy Park 6, Neagh Rd., Terenure 6, Orwell Quarry, Rathgar 6.

Dublin County Council Parks
Kilnamanagh, Dodder Park, Kingswood Heights, St. Mark's C.S., Tallaght C.S., Tallaght, Cherryfield, Walkinstown, Clondalkin Community Centre, Balally, Dundrum, Swords (behind the Castle), Skerries Community Centre, Balbriggan (rere of Church), Coolmine, Blanchardstown, Baltray, Howth, Seagrange, Baldoyle, Shankill, Meadowvale, Deansgrange.

Chapter 14
ARMCHAIR TRAVELLING

You may wish to get a more detailed history of Dublin, now that you've read this book. Here is a short list of good books on different aspects of the city. They should be in any library.

Guide to Historical Dublin by Adrian MacLoughlin (Gill and Macmillan). The best general guidebook.

The Neighbourhood of Dublin, Weston St. John Joyce (Gill and Macmillan). An old-fashioned book, full of gossip and stories, but most of his Dublin is now covered with our houses.

Encyclopaedia of Dublin by Douglas Bennett (Gill and Macmillan)

On Foot in Dublin and Wicklow Christopher Moriarty (Wolhound Press)

Dublin 1660-1860 by Maurice Craig (Hodges Figgis).

Dublin Tourism Handbook for up to date details.

Irish Youth Directory published by the National Youth Council.

Guide to Evening Classes in Dublin (Wolfhound Press).

Portmarnock: A Closer Look by Portmarnock Youth Project team (Wolfhound Press).

Joyce's Dublin: A Walking Guide to Ulysses by Jack McCarthy (Wolfhound Press).

Me Jewel & Darlin' Dublin by Eamonn MacThomáis (O'Brien Press).

Your Dinner's Poured Out! by Paddy Crosbie (O'Brien Press).

Medieval Dublin, Two Historic Walks Bride Rosney/Ian Broad (O'Brien Press in co-operation with the Friends of Medieval Dublin)